Delia's how to **cheat** at cooking.

dedication. This book is dedicated to specialist food suppliers everywhere. Thank you for helping us with our cooking and enriching our lives.

My heartfelt thanks go to a talented team of people without whom this book would not have been possible, especially Michael, my husband and taster-in-chief. Also to Brigette, our diligent ingredients specialist; Sarah, our outstanding editor; Vanessa, without doubt one of the best cookbook designers in the world; John, our wonderful photographer; Jo, enthusiastic and patient sub-editor; Pauline, the best tester of recipes ever; Melanie, without whom none of us could have pulled this off; Julia, whose help and support have played an enormous part and lastly, Debbie, my agent, who is still putting up with me after 39 years!

art direction & design. Vanessa Holden
photography. John Kernick
editor. Sarah Randell
pa to Delia Smith. Melanie Grocott
ingredients consultant. Brigette Hardy
sub editor. Jo Hill
recipe tester. Pauline Curran
additional food styling. Alison Attenborough

7 9 10 8 6

published in 2008 by Ebury Press, an imprint of Ebury Publishing, A Random House Group Company.

The Random House Group Limited Reg. No. 954009

addresses for companies within the Random House Group can be found at www.randomhouse.co.uk. A CIP catalogue record for this book is available from the British Library.

ISBN 978 0 091 92229 0

The Random House Group Limited makes every effort to ensure that the papers used in our books are made from trees that have been legally sourced from well-managed and credibly certified forests. Our paper procurement policy can be found on www.randomhouse.co.uk.

to buy books by your favourite authors and register for offers, visit www.rbooks.co.uk

colour origination by Altaimage, London

printed and bound in Italy by Graphicom, Srl

EBURY PRESS

Delia's
how to **cheat** at cooking.

contents.

introduction.

Welcome to How to Cheat at Cooking and a whole new approach to cooking and eating in the 21st century. Times have changed: almost imperceptibly our evolving lifestyle demands that, if not all of the time, then at least some of the time, we need a complete kitchen re-think.

Many of us love to cook when we have the time, but what happens when we don't? The challenge of how to eat well on a daily basis has not yet been met. We seem to have arrived at a kind of culinary dead end.

Young people are not taught to cook any more. Mums and dads both work but families still need feeding. A look around at what's on offer is not very edifying: expensive but ungenerous ready-meals, patchy takeaways and an absolute surfeit of addictive fat-laden, sugary snack foods that are pushing the nation towards an obesity crisis.

A look at your TV will reveal programmes that persist in ridiculing and humiliating people who can't cook (since they've never been taught), all the while perpetuating the myth that cooking skills belong to the privileged few.

What's on offer here is a way forward – first for those who are afraid to cook, and secondly, for those who are short of time. Cooking does not belong exclusively to professional chefs (TV or otherwise). Home cooking always has been, and always will be, something different and, if you short-circuit some of the accepted rules of cooking and are willing to explore alternatives by adding the cheating element, you can discover a better and easier way of coping when there's not much available time.

What our re-think here includes is a whole new way of shopping, which in turn leads to a different emphasis on storecupboard ingredients, as well as a complete sea-change on how the freezer is used – in that it now becomes an extension of the storecupboard.

Becoming a serious cheat can be very liberating. Without specific skills or precious time you can, whenever you want, produce spontaneous good food that's fun to prepare and free from anxiety. You can be sitting in your office planning your supper without going to a shop, or cook for your family and friends (and your children's friends) while still having time to enjoy being with them.

What's included in these pages is not going to win you any Michelin stars, but if you are afraid to cook or you're a very busy person, it will – at least some of the time – revolutionise your life. Interested? Read on.

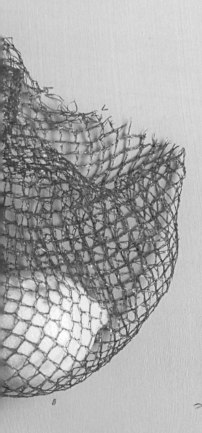

soups.

starters, light dishes & sides.

meat.

chicken.

the recipes.

fish & seafood.

vegetarian.

sweet endings.

general note. eggs used are large, free-range; butter is salted and spoon measurements are level, unless specified otherwise. We advise buying free-range chicken, and fish from sustainable sources. Product information correct at time of going to press.

a new way to shop...

If you want to cook and love to eat well, but have little time, what is contained in this book will help you. Everything here is geared to saving time but what it also needs is a completely fresh approach to how to shop.

The fridge, the storecupboard and the freezer have to be organised to serve you in a new, more considered way. If there are people out there dedicated to helping you save time, why not let them?

For instance, why not cut out grating cheese altogether when you're busy? There are now some good-quality ready-grated (or sliced) cheeses available: the finest Parmigiano Reggiano, mature Cheddar, even grated Gruyère (which has a beautiful melting quality in cooking) and for Italian dishes a mixture of ready-grated Cheddar and mozzarella. And let's not forget the versatile ready-made fresh cheese sauces, which also freeze very well.

There are ready-prepared and chopped vegetables, too, and a whole variety of prepared salads and fruits. The regular cheat keeps a sharp watch on all these, and stocks up – perhaps just once a week – to mix and match with the storecupboard and freezer. Your fridge can be home to real 'just like homemade' mayonnaise, to ready-cooked crisp smoked bacon, to crème fraîche which has a long shelf-life and can add that touch of richness to all kinds of dishes. The idea is, you do the cooking, but someone else has done the prep.

Like the fridge, the storecupboard can be stacked with treasures, not least good oils and vinegar to sprinkle on salads without the bother of making a dressing. So many wonderful ingredients are just waiting to make your life easier: ready-made ciabatta breadcrumbs, tins of fried Spanish onions, ginger already grated, pastry cases already cooked. In these pages I have tried to point you in the direction of some of the finest and best, but undoubtedly you will discover others once your cheat's antennae are attuned to this new kind of shopping.

It will involve tracking the shelves at your nearest supermarkets (in this scheme of things, loyalty to just one is out – because while there a lot available collectively, they all have some special ingredients that the others don't). It also means monitoring your local deli, specialist food shops or farm shops, where you not only get a more personal service but you can often order your favourite things specially. And don't forget the joy of armchair shopping online (see page 248).

If you invest in Asian storecupboard products you will always be able to transform ordinary ingredients very swiftly into something really special. Yes, it can seem a lot to acquire for just one recipe, but once you get into the habit with several recipes under your belt, you'll be hooked and forever grateful to have those extra-special ingredients on hand.

Last but not least, shopping for the freezer can be really liberating. Thanks to frozen diced onions, for instance, you're not forced to peel and chop an onion if you don't want to. Frozen foods allow you to cook spontaneously, free you from unnecessary trips to the shops and those frustrating experiences when you can't find what you want and empty spaces and out-of-stock signs are greeting you unsympathetically. If you like Thai food, for example, you will surely have experienced the sometimes futile search for ingredients in Asian shops. Now ingredients grown in Thailand are available deep-frozen in the UK in a complete recipe pack. It means that finding all the ingredients for an authentic Thai curry (page 134) merely involves a trip from your armchair to the freezer and you've got everything you need!

So it's under starter's orders. Off you go. I hope you will enjoy a new way of shopping and a new way of cooking and, most of all, I hope you have fun!

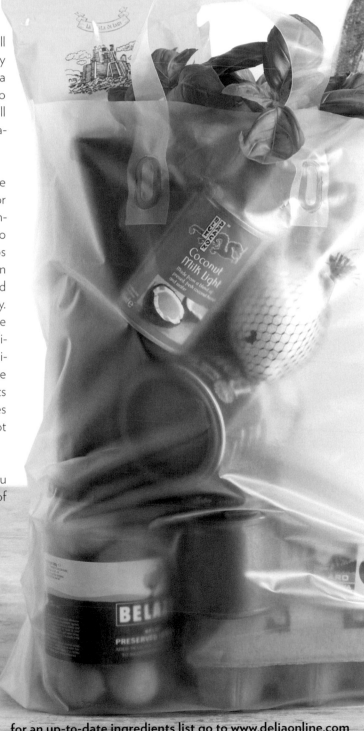

for an up-to-date ingredients list go to www.deliaonline.com

hidden servants.

In Victorian times, servants below stairs prepared food for the people living upstairs. But times have changed and today we are all living upstairs, and there are a million and one servants around the world beavering away, preparing quality foods designed to help us with our cooking at home.

Did you know that if you have no time to skin and chop tomatoes – let alone simmer and reduce them for hours to concentrate their flavour – someone south of Naples has done it all for you?

No time to peel and chop onions? What a break-through awaits you again. Someone in sunny Spain has peeled and chopped the finest Spanish onions and, what's more, gently softened them in olive oil, so you are left with your mascara intact.

Never again will your meringues crack and weep because now you can buy them as light as a whisper, made from only two ingredients – egg whites and sugar – and there are no worries about what on earth you are going to do with the yolks.

Oh, and yet another massive step for mankind. You no longer need endless jars of spices that have to be thrown out once a year – a couple of guys in Cheshire now import the finest spices from all round the world, then roast them and blend them into just the right combination for any country. So if you're feeling like Moroccan tonight and Goan tomorrow you've got it right there on your shelf in little re-sealable packs.

Once you've looked at the recipes and studied the top cheats list on page 246, all you need to do then is some smart shopping – probably once a month. It may mean going to more than one supermarket, or visits to delis, or sometimes shopping online. The aim is to build up your storecupboard to give you a range of choices at any given time.

Once you get a handle on this way of cooking you can sit smugly on your way home from work choosing what to cook tonight instead of agonising about getting to the shops.

cheats don't chop.

If you're short on time, forget about chopping boards, knife-sharpeners and the rest. Invest in a mini chopper (see page 50 and page 248 for stockists) for the price of about six cups of cappuccino, and you'll have the best little kitchen friend you could ever want. It is easier, more compact and reaches more places than its bigger brothers ever do. In fact, the recipes in this book have been devised to accommodate its smaller capacity. The other really useful item for the graduating cheat is a stick blender (see page 248 for stockists). Unless you actually enjoy cleaning out the goblet variety, this is so much easier: just whack it into the pan and press the button. Brilliant...

life from the freezer.

To say that cheating has come on a lot is an understatement, but nowhere has the revolution gained more momentum than in the whole area of freezing. The freezer – and how to use it – is absolutely fundamental to stress-free cooking.

Once you start learning how to cheat, the freezer becomes an extension of the storecupboard: you no longer cook for the freezer, you cook from it, you allow it (like the storecupboard) to provide you with any kind of meal you happen to feel like, at a moment's notice.

To begin with you have to rid yourself of prejudices, which sometimes are simply myths that have been perpetuated, or else a form of snobbery that maintains that frozen food is a bit down-market (witness the empty aisles in the freezer section in otherwise packed supermarkets). What needs to be said is that the freezer section has within it buried treasures that will give you an easier life overnight without – most important of all – going short on quality.

With modern techniques of blast-freezing, the 'freshness' of foods is not impaired. Fish is frozen at sea, so why buy it ready de-frosted? Once vegetables are harvested, they begin to lose their nutritional value the longer they hang about. Just think how many fresh foods you have thrown out because of the wretched sell-by dates.

Cheats are liberated from sell-by dates. What do you feel like cooking and eating tonight? All you have to do is choose. And one of the bonuses of the freezer revolution is – in very many cases – not having to de-frost. Indeed, the eating quality of frozen foods is often better when they are actually cooked from frozen.

As you turn the pages of this book you'll discover things you hadn't dreamed of. You'll never have to peel and prepare potatoes if you're busy. Rice – brown, white, basmati – comes in measured portions. You can now buy frozen, ready-cooked chickpeas and red kidney beans, chargrilled slices of aubergine, ready-diced onions, Australian snapper fillets, all kinds of seafood, artichoke hearts, ready-rolled pastry-lined tart cases (large or individual), risotto made in Italy ready to serve in four minutes...

Once you move into getting your storecupboard and freezer up to speed, you will be able to produce a whole range of meals quite spontaneously and, most important of all, very quickly.

who peels the
potatoes?

anyone but you!

cracked potatoes with melting cheese & spring onions.

Everyone who tries these roast potatoes loves them and this recipe just adds an extra dimension – great served with gammon steaks.

700g	Aunt Bessie's Homestyle frozen crispy roast potatoes
50g	ready-grated Gruyère (Tesco and Asda)
2	tablespoons fresh ready-grated Parmesan
4	spring onions, including the green parts, chopped

Pre-heat the oven to gas mark 9, 240°C. Roast the potatoes on a lightly greased medium baking tray on a high shelf in the oven for 25-30 minutes and, after 20 minutes, pre-heat the grill to its highest setting.

When the potatoes are cooked, cut any really large ones in half, then, with a large fork, press firmly down on all of them (to 'crack' them slightly). Now scatter the spring onions over the potatoes, then sprinkle on the grated Gruyère. Finally, dust the whole lot with the Parmesan and a seasoning of pepper. Place under the grill for 3-4 minutes until the cheese has browned and is bubbling.

note: for a variation you could use different cheeses or add 75g cubed pancetta – scatter it among the potatoes once they have been roasting for 15 minutes.

serves 4.

shortcut omelette Savoyard.

This is one of our old favourites, which we've speeded up with the help of a few cheats' ingredients. A truly brilliant fast lunch or late supper dish. If you prefer, instead of ready-grated Gruyère, you can use the same quantity of Gruyère slices.

4	eggs, beaten
390g	tin Eazy fried onions
2	McCain frozen potato rosti, defrosted for about 30 minutes
1	pack (about 50g) ready-cooked crispy smoked bacon
1	dessertspoon olive oil
50g	ready-grated Gruyère (Tesco and Asda)

Start off by pre-heating the grill to its highest setting and draining the onions in a sieve set over a bowl. Next, crumble the rosti into a mixing bowl and add the crispy bacon (also crumbled), followed by the drained onions. Then give them all a good mix.

Next, heat the oil in a medium non-stick frying-pan, then add the potato rosti mixture and let it cook over a medium heat for about 5 minutes, stirring it around so it doesn't catch. After that, sprinkle in three-quarters of the grated Gruyère, turn the heat up, season the eggs, then pour them into the pan. Now, using a palette knife, draw the outside of the omelette inwards for about a minute to allow the liquid egg to escape to the edges. Then sprinkle over the rest of the grated cheese.

Now transfer the pan to the grill, about 10cm from the heat, for 2-3 minutes to set the top of the omelette. Let it settle for a couple of minutes then serve, cut into wedges, with a side salad.

serves 2.

potato, Roquefort & sage bread.

Bread? Cheats? Yes, it takes hardly any time to make and is a hundred times better than anything you can buy.

2	McCain frozen potato rosti, defrosted for about 30 minutes
50g	Roquefort (or any strong-flavoured cheese)
1	dessertspoon chopped fresh sage, plus 6 fresh sage leaves
175g	self-raising flour, plus extra for dusting
1	teaspoon salt
¼	teaspoon cayenne pepper
1	teaspoon English mustard powder
1	heaped tablespoon cottage cheese with chives
1	egg, beaten with 2 tablespoons milk

Pre-heat the oven to gas mark 5, 190°C. First, using your hands, crumble the defrosted rosti into shreds in a bowl, then crumble half the Roquefort cheese in to join it. Now sift the flour, salt, cayenne and mustard powder into the bowl, then add the cottage cheese and chopped sage.

Next, add the beaten egg and milk then, using a palette knife, mix everything together and finally bring it together with your hands to form a rough, loose dough. Shape it into a ball, place it on a greased baking sheet, then flatten it slightly. Arrange the sage leaves in a circle on top, sprinkle with the rest of the Roquefort, crumbled (pressing it into the dough), and dust with a little extra flour.

Bake the bread on the centre shelf of the oven for 35-40 minutes till golden-brown, then remove it to a wire rack to cool a little. This is best eaten fresh and still warm with butter, but next day it is also good toasted –*and* it freezes well.

makes 1 loaf (to serve 4-6).

hot smoked salmon & quail egg pie.

This ticks all the boxes for casual entertaining with friends – seriously yum and hardly any work. If you don't want to use quails' eggs, three hardboiled hen's eggs will do just fine.

4	hot smoked salmon fillets (2 x 160g packs)
12	(120g pack) Aperi Quail cooked peeled quail eggs, whole or halved
6-8	cornichons, sliced
1	rounded tablespoon capers, rinsed and drained
2	tablespoons chopped fresh dill
	juice of 1 lemon
1	tub (300g or 350g) ready-prepared fresh cheese sauce
1	rounded tablespoon half-fat crème fraîche
12-16	discs Aunt Bessie's Homestyle frozen mashed potato
1½-2	heaped tablespoons ready-grated mature Cheddar
1	heaped tablespoon ready-grated Parmesan
	cayenne pepper
	watercress, to garnish

Pre-heat the oven to gas mark 6, 200°C. We used a dish about 18cm square for this but an oval one of similar size would do. The skin of the salmon will peel off very easily, then just break it up into largish pieces and place them in the dish. After that, scatter in the quails' eggs, cornichons, capers, dill and lemon juice, and add a seasoning of salt. Next, whisk the cheese sauce with the crème fraîche and pour that all over the fish.

Now, arrange the frozen mashed potato discs on top, overlapping them in rows. Follow that with the Cheddar, the Parmesan and a sprinkling of cayenne. Bake on a highish shelf in the oven for 30-40 minutes until the top is golden-brown and the sauce is bubbling. Let it settle out of the oven for 10 minutes before serving garnished with watercress. Fresh ready-shelled peas would be a good accompaniment, or a salad with a lemony dressing (Waitrose Amaranth & Watercress salad, available from May-September, is brilliant).

serves 4.

23

oven–sautéed potatoes with red onion, garlic & rosemary.

A pack of frozen spuds becomes really classy with this treatment; the finishing flourish is a sprinkling of rosemary flaked sea salt.

300g	McCain frozen crispy slices
1	red onion, peeled, halved and thinly sliced
1	clove garlic, peeled and chopped small
1	tablespoon chopped fresh rosemary
2	teaspoons extra virgin olive oil
	rosemary flaked sea salt (Tesco)

Pre-heat the oven to gas mark 8, 230°C. Put the frozen potato slices in a bowl and toss them around in 1 teaspoon of the olive oil, then spread them out in a single layer on a baking sheet and pop them in the oven for 10 minutes. Meanwhile, toss the onion, garlic and rosemary in the other teaspoon of oil in the same bowl, then after the 10 minutes is up, sprinkle this mixture over the potatoes (holding the baking sheet with a cloth as you do this). Then slide it back into the oven for a further 20 minutes. Serve the potatoes sprinkled with rosemary flaked sea salt and freshly milled black pepper.

serves 2.

patatas bravas.

My favourite tapas bar in London, Mar i Terra, inspired this recipe – so go there if you want the real thing. My take on it is pretty brilliant even if I say so myself – provided you've got proper Delouis Fils fresh mayonnaise for the sauce.

300g   **McCain frozen crispy bites**
1   **dessertspoon extra virgin olive oil, preferably Spanish**
2   **fat cloves garlic, peeled, or 3 smaller ones**
2   **heaped tablespoons Delouis Fils fresh mayonnaise**
1   **dessertspoon white wine vinegar (Tesco Finest Chardonnay white wine vinegar is good)**
2   **heaped teaspoons La Chinata or El Avion hot smoked Spanish paprika**
      Maldon sea salt flakes

Pre-heat the oven to gas mark 8, 230°C. Toss the frozen crispy bites in the olive oil (to give them that authentic Spanish flavour), then place them on a baking tray. Bake on a high shelf in the oven for 25-30 minutes, or until very crisp.

Meanwhile, crush the garlic and ½ teaspoon salt flakes to a paste in a pestle and mortar, then mix it with the mayonnaise, wine vinegar and paprika. When the potatoes are cooked, remove them to a cold serving plate and let them cool a little (they need to be warm rather than hot). Then spoon the sauce here and there over them and serve with other tapas or as a side dish to a main course.

serves 4-6 as part of a tapas selection or 2 as a side dish.

luxury seafood pie.

This is for 'treat yourself' time, so buy a piece of skinned and filleted monkfish tail – the prawns and scallops can come from the freezer. A lovely recipe to serve to friends.

450g	prepared monkfish or other firm white fish
225g	frozen peeled raw tiger or king prawns
200g	frozen scallops
150ml	dry vermouth
3	tablespoons chopped fresh dill
10	cornichons
1	well-heaped tablespoon capers, rinsed and drained
1	tub (300g or 350g) ready-prepared fresh cheese sauce
650g	Aunt Bessie's Homestyle frozen mashed potato
3	rounded tablespoons fresh, ready-grated Parmesan cayenne pepper

Pre-heat the oven to gas mark 7, 220°C. Start off by placing the frozen prawns and scallops in a large frying-pan with the vermouth and some seasoning, bring it up to a gentle simmer, cover and give it 5 minutes. After that, remove the prawns and scallops from the cooking liquid, turn the heat up and let it boil vigorously without a lid till reduced to about 2 tablespoons.

Now arrange the prawns, scallops (halved if large) and the raw monkfish or other fish (divided into largish chunks) in a baking dish measuring about 18cm x 23cm. Slice the cornichons into rounds, then sprinkle these, the dill and the capers all over the fish.

Sprinkle over the reduced vermouth and add some seasoning, then the cheese sauce. Finally, arrange the frozen potato discs, slightly overlapping, over the top, and finish off with the Parmesan sprinkled evenly all over and a dusting of cayenne pepper. Bake the pie on a high shelf for 40 minutes and let it settle out of the oven for 10 minutes before serving.

serves 6.

anyone for brunch?

chilli eggs with roasted peppers

*oven–sautéed potatoes
with red onion, garlic & rosemary*

capers in the larder

not the naughty sort.

chilli eggs with roasted peppers.

We have found that this makes an excellent brunch or supper dish for one simply by halving the ingredients.

4	eggs
285g	jar roasted red and yellow peppers in oil (M&S), drained (but reserve the oil)
4	pieces jalapeño pepper, from a jar
1	medium onion, peeled and quartered
1	large clove garlic, peeled
400g	tin Italian chopped tomatoes, drained
12	pitted black Kalamata olives (Sainsbury's, or other)

Pre-heat the grill to its highest setting. First, chop the onion, garlic and jalapeño pepper in a mini-chopper (not too finely), then heat 1 dessertspoon of the oil, reserved from the peppers, in a frying-pan and add the chopped ingredients. Soften them for 5 minutes or so till they take on some colour. Meanwhile, slice the drained roasted peppers into smallish strips.

Now pour the drained chopped tomatoes into the pan to join the onions, followed by the strips of roasted pepper and, finally, sprinkle in the olives. Season, give it all a good stir and continue to cook for a further 5 minutes. Then move the pepper mixture to the edge of the pan, making a space in the centre.

Break the eggs into the space, season and then cook over a medium heat for 4 minutes before transferring the frying-pan to the preheated grill – approximately 10cm from the heat. Cook until the eggs are set to your liking, but do keep a close eye on them because things can happen quite quickly at this stage.

serves 2.

lobster & coconut soup with lemongrass & ginger.

Here we've got a ready-made soup as a backdrop – so no initial work needed, just a little tinkering around with some other very fine ingredients, which puts it in a different class.

415g	tin lobster bisque, such as Baxters
165ml	tin Blue Dragon light coconut milk
1	stalk Blue Dragon whole lemongrass (from a jar)
1	heaped dessertspoon English Provender very lazy ginger
1	dessertspoon Thai fish sauce
1	tablespoon lime juice, plus a little more if needed
1	heaped tablespoon fresh coriander leaves

You have some work to do, but not much: just cut the lemongrass into 3 pieces and chop them in a mini-chopper with the ginger as finely as possible. What happens now is the lobster bisque and the coconut milk are emptied into a medium saucepan, along with the lemongrass and ginger, and stirred around. Then, keeping the heat on low, leave it to heat very gently, uncovered, for 10 minutes, without coming to the boil.

Finally – making sure the soup is now hot – add the fish sauce and lime juice (taste to see if it needs more lime), then serve in warmed soup bowls with the coriander to garnish.

serves 2, or 4 as a starter.

Mexican black bean soup.

This is unbelievably good and takes only 20 minutes. Why not pre-heat the grill while it is cooking and serve it with tortillas topped with melted cheese (ready-sliced or ready-grated), then halved and folded? Just a thought.

400g	tin Epicure black beans
1	small red onion, peeled and quartered
1	clove garlic, peeled
4	rashers smoked pancetta (Sainsbury's or Tesco) or bacon, snipped in half
1	teaspoon olive oil
½	teaspoon cumin seeds
4 or 5	sprigs fresh coriander
425ml	hot vegetable stock made from Marigold bouillon powder
	Tabasco sauce
1	dessertspoon lime juice
1	rounded dessertspoon half-fat crème fraîche

Pulse the onion, garlic and pancetta together in a mini-chopper till chopped small. Next, heat the oil in a medium saucepan, add the chopped ingredients along with the cumin seeds and sauté gently for about 5 minutes.

Meanwhile, rinse the black beans in a sieve under the cold tap and add them to the saucepan along with the coriander stalks (keep the leaves till later). Add the stock and a few drops of Tabasco, simmer for 5 minutes, then cover the pan and simmer for a further 5 minutes.

Finally, purée the soup with a stick blender, then add the reserved coriander leaves, the lime juice and some seasoning. Serve in warmed soup bowls with a swirl of crème fraîche.

serves 2, or 4 as a starter.

Mediterranean fish stew.

This is a sort of bouillabaisse. When I saw snapper fillets in the freezer at Tesco, I knew there had to be some kind of cheats' version of a fish stew there. So, courtesy of a jar of fish soup and some other lovely seafood, here we are. In Provence they often serve bouillabaisse with dollops of rouille stirred in: if you want to go the whole hog, the recipe is on page 66.

500g	frozen Australian snapper fillets (Tesco Finest), or other firm white fish
200g	frozen small roeless scallops
200g	frozen mixed raw seafood or fruits de mer from a pack (such as prawns, squid and mussels)
850ml	jar Perard du Touquet soupe de poissons (see page 248 for stockists)
4	tablespoons dry vermouth
1	tablespoon fresh chopped parsley

Begin by emptying the contents of the jar of soup into a large, flameproof casserole, rinse out the jar with the vermouth and add that, then bring it all up to a gentle simmer. Add the frozen snapper fillets and poach them gently in the liquid for about 15 minutes.

After that, add the frozen scallops and mixed seafood and poach them for 5-7 minutes (keeping the fish submerged in the liquid) or until cooked through. Taste and season, then serve in warm shallow bowls, placing the snapper fillets in the centre and spooning the rest of the fish and sauce on top and around. Sprinkle with parsley, and the traditional accompaniment is tiny boiled potatoes.

serves 4.

39

Creole prawns.

As Creole cooking only ever uses green peppers (and the colour's nice), I've included a fresh pepper here. Otherwise, the equivalent amount from a jar of roasted peppers can be used without detracting from the end result.

250g	frozen raw tiger or king prawns
1	large onion, peeled and quartered
1	fat clove garlic, peeled
1	green pepper
1	tablespoon olive oil
350g	jar Dress Italian tomato sauce with red pepper and chilli
150ml	dry white wine
2	spring onions, including the green parts, finely chopped

Start by chopping the onion and garlic in a mini-chopper and de-seed and slice the pepper into smallish strips. Then heat the oil in a medium frying-pan over a highish heat, add the chopped onion and garlic and the sliced pepper and, moving them around, give them 5 minutes to begin to soften and colour.

After that, add the frozen prawns and stir them around for about 5 minutes, until they start to turn pink on both sides. Now pour in the sauce, use the white wine to rinse out the jar (shake it with the lid on), then add that too to the pan, along with some seasoning. Bring to the boil, give a good stir, then turn the heat down to its lowest setting and let it simmer gently for 5 minutes. Scatter with the spring onions and serve with rice, pasta, noodles or couscous – however the mood takes you.

serves 2.

wild salmon & caper fishcakes with watercress mayonnaise.

I have long held – even without my cheating hat on – that tinned salmon makes the best fishcakes, even more so if it's tinned wild salmon. In summer this is good with Watercress Mayonnaise, and in winter with the No-Panic Hollandaise (see page 79) combined with some chopped watercress.

213g	tin wild salmon
1	rounded dessertspoon capers, rinsed and drained
4	discs Aunt Bessie's Homestyle frozen mashed potato
85g	bag watercress
2	good-sized cornichons, chopped
3	good pinches cayenne pepper
1	rounded tablespoon semolina
1	tablespoon groundnut or other flavourless oil
2	lemon wedges

FOR WATERCRESS MAYONNAISE

2	rounded tablespoons Delouis Fils fresh mayonnaise, mixed with 1 dessertspoon lemon juice chopped watercress (see method)

Begin by defrosting the mashed potato – 2 minutes in a microwave or in a saucepan over a medium heat, then cool. After that, drain the tinned salmon well in a sieve, pressing it down with the back of a spoon. Then place the salmon in a mixing bowl, along with the potato.

Next, chop three-quarters of the bag of watercress in a mini-chopper and add a tablespoon of the chopped watercress to the bowl, along with the cornichons and capers. Add some salt and the cayenne, and give everything a good mix with a fork. Now spoon the semolina on to a plate, then divide the salmon mixture into 6 and shape them into rounds, using your hands and coating each one with semolina as you go.

To cook, heat the oil in a large frying-pan and, when it is very hot and slightly shimmering, add the fishcakes and cook them briefly – about 2 minutes on each side. For the watercress mayonnaise, stir the lemon juice and the remaining chopped watercress into the mayonnaise and season. Serve with the fishcakes and garnish with the rest of the watercress from the bag and lemon wedges to squeeze over.

serves 2.

Moroccan grilled fish with pineapple salsa.

Because of the marinade this is best made with defrosted frozen or fresh fish, rather than cooking the fish from frozen.

| 2 | thick skinless cod or haddock fillets, 175-200g each (use sustainable fish from Icelandic or Pacific waters) |

FOR THE MARINADE

1	Belazu preserved lemon, quartered
1	piece jalapeño pepper, from a jar
	pinch of saffron strands, crumbled
1	clove garlic, peeled
½	teaspoon paprika
	juice of ½ lemon
1	tablespoon olive oil
1	dessertspoon each fresh parsley and coriander leaves

FOR THE PINEAPPLE SALSA

6	pieces from a pack of ready-prepared fresh pineapple
1-2	pieces jalapeño pepper, from a jar
½	small red onion, peeled
1	dessertspoon fresh coriander

Just pile the marinade ingredients into a mini-chopper and whiz them to a coarse purée. Now place the fish fillets in a shallow heatproof dish, season with salt, then spread the marinade over both sides. Cover the dish and leave on one side for up to 30 minutes at room temperature. The salsa ingredients can now go into the same mini-chopper (no need to wash it first). Pulse till just evenly chopped, then spoon into a serving bowl.

To cook the fish: pre-heat the grill to its highest setting for 10 minutes. Place the fish about 10cm from the heat source and grill it for 10 minutes or until golden and cooked through. Nice served with something green, like rocket, with any escaped juices spooned over, and the salsa. Great on its own or with couscous.

serves 2.

bonfire steaks with Mexican tomato salsa.

This is so very good we're serving it at Yellows, our American diner at the football club. It's a sublime combination of Mexican spice and flavours with a hint of chocolate.

2	rib-eye steaks (Asda Extra Special)
1	tablespoon olive oil
1	tablespoon bonfire rub (Asda Extra Special)
	Maldon sea salt
	dressed salad leaves, such as ruby salad (Asda Extra Special)

FOR THE MEXICAN TOMATO SALSA

2	large, firm tomatoes
½	medium red onion, peeled and quartered
	about 1 tablespoon fresh coriander leaves
	zest and juice of ½ lime

All you need do is combine the oil with the bonfire rub in a small bowl, then spread this mixture on both sides of the steaks. If you have time they can be left to marinate; if not, they will still be good.

For the salsa, pour boiling water over the tomatoes and after 1 minute drain them and slip the skins off. Then cut them in half and squeeze out the seeds. Add the tomato flesh to a mini-chopper along with the rest of the ingredients, then pulse-chop them (but not too finely).

When you're ready to cook the steaks, pre-heat the grill to its highest setting for about 10 minutes. Whack them under the hot grill, about 10cm from the heat and cook them for about 4-5 minutes on each side – 5-6 if you like steak well-done. When cooked, place them on a board, sprinkle with sea salt and slice them into thin strips, then pile them on top of the dressed salad leaves and serve with the Mexican tomato salsa.

serves 2.

plaice fillets with shrimp sauce.

Any fish can be used for this, but frozen plaice fillets or Greek farmed sea bass are particularly good. As this is such a whiz of a quick supper it is good to have potted shrimps to hand. If you use defrosted or fresh fish, cut the grilling time to 5–6 minutes.

4	frozen plaice fillets (Waitrose) or Greek farmed sea bass fillets (Waitrose or Tesco)
2	pots (each 57g) Marine Gourmet or other Morecambe Bay brown potted shrimps (see page 248 for stockists)
2	generous pinches ground mace
1	generous pinch cayenne pepper
2	tablespoons dry vermouth
1	tablespoon half-fat crème fraîche
1	tablespoon fresh chopped parsley

Begin by pre-heating the grill to its highest setting for about 10 minutes.

Meanwhile, empty the potted shrimps into a small frying-pan and place it over a low heat so the butter from the shrimps gently melts. After that, spoon off about half the melted butter in a saucer and remove the pan from the heat.

Now line a grill rack with foil and brush it with some of the reserved butter. Next place the frozen fish fillets (flesh side up) side by side on the foil, brush them with more of the butter and season. Place the grill pan about 10cm from the heat and grill the fish for 10-12 minutes until the flesh is opaque and the surface golden-brown.

While that's happening, place the shrimps back on the heat, add the ground mace, cayenne and some salt, and when the butter begins to sizzle add the vermouth. Let it bubble for 1 minute, then stir in the crème fraîche. Let that bubble for about half a minute, then remove from the heat and stir in the parsley. Serve spooned over the cooked fish fillets.

serves 2.

47

grilled fish with red pepper & walnut pesto.

We recently served this with Waitrose frozen artichoke hearts (see page 162). Thus a meal for 2 was ready in 45 minutes flat from the freezer to the table.

4	frozen Greek farmed sea bass fillets (Waitrose or Tesco)
180g	jar Dress Italian red pepper and walnut pesto
	little olive oil, for brushing
1	tablespoon pitted black Kalamata olives (Sainsbury's or other)
1	tablespoon capers, rinsed and drained
	small handful fresh basil leaves, shredded

Begin this one by pre-heating the grill to its highest setting for at least 10 minutes. While that's happening, line a grill pan with foil and brush it with olive oil.

Then empty the contents of the jar of pesto into a bowl. Now lay the frozen fillets flesh side down on the foil and brush them with some of the surplus oil from the pesto. After that, place the grill pan 10cm from the heat and time the fish for 5 minutes. Meanwhile, slice the olives and combine with the capers.

Then turn the fillets over carefully, brush the other side with a little more oil from the pesto and give them another 5 minutes. Then pour the pesto over the fish fillets and scatter the sliced olives and whole capers over that. Grill for another 2-3 minutes, then serve with the basil sprinkled over.

serves 2.

Black Forest ham & lentil soup.

The secret of this old favourite, made simpler and speedier with tinned lentils, is the lovely smoky flavour of the ham.

75g	Black Forest ham slices, cut into strips
400g	tin Epicure organic lentils, or similar
1	medium carrot, peeled
1	medium onion, peeled
1	celery stalk
1	clove garlic, peeled
1	dessertspoon olive oil
570ml	hot vegetable stock made from Marigold bouillon powder
230g	tin Italian chopped tomatoes
100g	ready-prepared shredded cabbage

You can make light work of chopping the vegetables (except for the cabbage) by using the mini-chopper. So pop them in, cut into chunks, along with the garlic and strips of ham, then whiz till everything is finely diced.

Now all you do is heat the oil in a large pan, add the chopped vegetables and ham and toss them around uncovered – with the heat high – until they brown a little at the edges (about 3-4 minutes). Then drain and rinse the lentils and add these, together with the stock and tinned tomatoes plus some seasoning, and simmer with a lid on for 10 minutes.

Then, after the 10 minutes are up, add the shredded cabbage to the rest of the ingredients and continue to simmer, covered, for a further 5 minutes. Serve in warmed soup bowls.

serves 2-3, or 4 as a starter.

laid-back
lunches
lighter stuff.

for an up-to-date ingredients list go to www.deliaonline.com

meze plate.

One easy no-cook impromptu way to serve 6 people is to always have a stock of Odysea Greek meze in the cupboard. These are superb quality, made authentically in Greece and their frozen pitta bread is miles better than the wangy English stuff.

150g	diced Greek feta with extra virgin olive oil and oregano (M&S),or any crumbled feta
2-3	large firm tomatoes, quartered
20cm	piece cucumber, halved lengthways and sliced
	juice of 1 lemon
	olive oil
220g	jar Odysea aubergine meze
340g	jar Odysea stuffed vine leaves
	a few Karyatis mixed hot chillies (from a jar)
	Odysea frozen authentic Greek pitta bread, to serve

Pre-heat the grill. To cook the pitta bread from frozen, sprinkle it with water and a few drops of olive oil, then heat it under the grill for a few minutes on each side. Meanwhile, in a bowl, toss together the feta, tomatoes and cucumber with the lemon juice, 2 tablespoons olive oil and some freshly milled black pepper. Empty the contents of the jars of aubergine meze and vine leaves, plus a few chillies, into serving dishes and serve with the salad and hot pitta for everyone to help themselves to.

serves 6.

Michael's club sandwich.

My husband Michael has always been an ace sandwich maker (in fact, he is now an accomplished cook). After a long-distance away match, we find this fits the bill perfectly.

6	thin slices white bread, from a large good-quality loaf
1	ready-cooked chicken breast
	soft butter
1	generous handful watercress, spinach and rocket salad (tough stalks removed)
2	medium tomatoes, thinly sliced
½	medium red onion, thinly sliced, or 4 spring onions, chopped
4	generous dessertspoons Delouis Fils fresh mayonnaise
1	pack (about 50g) ready-cooked crispy smoked bacon
1	small avocado, peeled, halved, stoned and thinly sliced
8	cornichons

You're also going to need 8 toothpicks. Start off by toasting the bread lightly on both sides and, while that's happening, slice the chicken breast as thinly as possible. Then let the toast cool in a rack to keep it crisp before buttering 4 of the slices.

For the first sandwich, place one piece of toast, buttered side up, on a board and arrange a few of the salad leaves on top. Then add half the tomato slices and sliced or chopped onions and season well. Next, spread a generous dessertspoon of mayonnaise over the onion, then crumble the crispy bacon and sprinkle half of it over the mayonnaise.

Now, place one of the unbuttered pieces of toast on top, followed by half the slices of chicken. Spread another dessertspoon of mayonnaise over that, followed by half the slices of avocado and a few more salad leaves. Season, then top with another buttered piece of toast.

Spear 4 cornichons with toothpicks, then press the toothpicks through the sandwich, one near each corner. Cut the sandwich into 4, using gentle sawing movements (and not pressing down too hard!). Repeat the same process for the other sandwich – Michael likes them served with Kettle chips.

serves 2.

56

eggs Benedict.

This is the ultimate snack for a lunch, a brunch or a late light supper. Now that we have the cheats' version of Hollandaise, it's made in moments.

4	**eggs**
2	**English muffins**
1	**pack (about 50g) ready-cooked crispy smoked bacon or**
	4 slices Black Forest ham
	soft butter
1	**quantity of warm No-panic Hollandaise (see page 79)**

First, preheat the grill. Then bring a small frying-pan of water to just below simmering point (ie when small bubbles begin to form on the base). Now carefully break the eggs into it, let them cook gently for 1 minute, then remove the frying-pan from the heat, put a lid on and let the eggs finish cooking for a further 6 minutes.

Meanwhile, split the muffins horizontally and toast them on both sides, then place them on the floor of the grill to keep warm. Next warm the bacon (or ham) through under the hot grill for a few seconds, generously butter the muffins and top each one with the bacon or ham, followed by the poached eggs (use a draining spoon and a wodge of kitchen paper underneath to soak up any excess moisture). Finally, pour the Hollandaise sauce over the eggs, return the dish to the grill for about a minute, then serve straightaway.

serves 2.

calamares fritos.
fried baby squid.

These are so simple – they take seconds to cook and are good served with Tracklements' Chilli Jam. I buy mine ready-prepared (still frozen from the fish counter at Waitrose) so I can always have a stash in the freezer.

200g	frozen baby squid, defrosted at room temperature for about 20 minutes
2-3	tablespoons olive oil
2	egg whites
2	tablespoons plain flour
	Maldon sea salt
	Tracklements chilli jam, to serve

Pull out the frilly bits tucked inside the baby squid and reserve, then dry the whole lot well with kitchen paper. Next, slice the elongated part of the squid into small rings.

Heat 2 tablespoons of oil until very hot in a small frying-pan and, while it's heating, whisk the egg whites till stiff. Now dip all the pieces of squid first in the flour then in the egg white, and fry them in the hot oil (turning them over) for about 45 seconds cooking time in all. You'll need to do this in two batches, topping up with a little more oil if necessary. Drain them on kitchen paper and serve quickly, sprinkled with Maldon sea salt and freshly milled black pepper, with chilli jam alongside.

serves 2 as a starter or part of a tapas selection.

antipasti.

Where's the cheating? But look, there's no cooking at all, just a bit of smart shopping and you've got something really good to serve for lunch or a light supper.

150g   sliced Milano or finocchio (fennel) salami
150g   Parma ham (Sainsbury's Taste the Difference
         24-month matured Parma ham is best)
150g   mortadella, in slices
250g   taleggio cheese, sliced
         cornichons
         pitted black Kalamata olives (Sainsbury's, or other)
         Delicias green chilli peppers or Fruttibosco antipasto
         (see left, and page 248 for stockists)

In essence this just involves a large platter on which you arrange the slices of salami, Parma ham and mortadella, along with the slices of taleggio. Then tucked in amongst it all some cornichons, olives and perhaps a few mild green chillies , or a jar of antipasto to serve alongside.

Serve with breadsticks, warmed focaccia or ciabatta bread, and have a dish of really good extra virgin olive oil to dip into.

serves 6.

a salad of pears with walnuts & Roquefort dressing.

This salad is also great as a starter and the dressing, which can be made with other blue cheese such as Gorgonzola, is good with any chunky salad.

420g	jar pear quarters in grape juice (M&S), or any tinned pears
25g	walnut halves
110g	watercress, spinach and rocket salad
4	spring onions, including the green parts, finely chopped

FOR THE ROQUEFORT DRESSING

40g	Roquefort
2	rounded tablespoons half-fat crème fraîche
2	rounded tablespoons Delouis Fils fresh mayonnaise
1	fat clove garlic, peeled
1	teaspoon English mustard powder
1	tablespoon Fattorie Giacobazzi vintage aged balsamic vinegar (Sainsbury's)

Divide the salad among the serving plates and scatter over the spring onions, then drain the pears in a sieve and dry them a little with kitchen paper before arranging them on top of the salad. Place the walnuts in a mini-chopper and pulse-chop them until quite chunky, then empty them on to a plate.

For the dressing: add all the ingredients to the mini-chopper, season with freshly milled black pepper and whiz till the mixture is almost smooth – a few little bits of cheese left give it an interesting texture. Drizzle the dressing over the pears and scatter the walnuts over. Walnut bread would be great served with this.

serves 4, or 6 as a starter.

caramelised onion & taleggio tartlets.

This would be a very laid-back lunch indeed – hardly any worry at all – or equally, it could be a wonderfully easy first course if you're entertaining.

200g	jar English Provender very lazy caramelised red onions, drained
250g	taleggio cheese
6	savoury pastry tartlet cases (M&S)
1	tablespoon chopped fresh sage, plus 6 small leaves
1	dessertspoon Fattorie Giacobazzi vintage aged balsamic vinegar (Sainsbury's)
	olive oil, for drizzling

Pre-heat the oven to gas mark 4, 180°C. Start off by mixing the onions, vinegar and chopped sage in a bowl and season them. Then place the tartlet cases on a medium-size baking tray and divide the onion mixture among them.

After that, remove the rind from the taleggio with a sharp knife and cut the cheese into 18 slices (it doesn't matter if they are not perfect slices). Arrange 3 of these on the top of each tartlet, overlapping and slightly covering the edge of the pastry. Place a sage leaf in the centre of each tartlet, then season and drizzle a little olive oil over. Bake the tartlets in the centre of the oven for 15 minutes and serve them warm, with a garnish of dressed salad leaves.

serves 6.

gambas pil pil.
prawns in sizzling garlic & chilli oil.

The best gambas pil pil we've ever tasted was in a scruffy little café in the square of a back-of-beyond town in central Spain. After sampling it many more times throughout Spain, nothing could better it – until now. You won't believe something so simple and made in moments could taste so sublime.

12	frozen peeled raw tiger or king prawns
2	fat cloves garlic, peeled and thinly sliced
2	piri piri chillies, from a jar (Tesco Ingredients or Waitrose Cooks' Ingredients), stalks removed and chopped small
4	tablespoons olive oil
	lots of crusty bread or baguette

What is essential here is a small heatproof dish (preferably terracotta and about 12cm in diameter). Begin by pre-heating the grill and the dish by placing it 10cm from the heat. Now measure 1 tablespoon of the oil into a small frying-pan and the rest of the oil into a small saucepan. Place the frying-pan on a high heat and, when the oil is hot and shimmering, add the prawns and stir them in the hot oil for 2 minutes or until they are completely pink and opaque on both sides, then remove from the heat.

Next, heat the oil in the saucepan and, when that too is shimmering hot, use a spatula to transfer the prawns and all the juicy oil to the saucepan, followed by the garlic and chopped chillies (use a tablespoon for this). Let it all sizzle for 1 minute – the garlic needs to be golden but not brown. Now, using oven gloves, remove the very hot dish from the grill, scoop the prawns and their oil into it, and take it to the table still sizzling.

Dip pieces of bread into the oil and scoop a prawn along with a slice of garlic and a fleck of chilli. And don't forget, even the flavoured oil left in the bottom of the dish absolutely must be absorbed in the bread and eaten.

note: for a light lunch or starter, double the quantities and use 2 bowls.

serves 2 as part of a tapas selection.

65

soupe de poissons (with the works!)

Every coastal region in France has its own Soupe de Poissons made from a variety of fresh fish and shellfish. This one, made in Le Touquet and sold in jars over here, is so very good perhaps they are all made from it! The 'works' involves grated Gruyère, baked croûtons and a dollop of very garlicky rouille sauce. The first two are obligingly supplied ready-made, and the rouille takes about 1 minute to make. It has never failed to please.

FOR THE SOUP

850ml jar	Perard du Touquet soupe de poissons (see page 248 for stockists)
170g	tin jumbo crab meat (Asda Extra Special), or other white crab meat, drained
43g	tin John West dressed lobster meat, drained
1	heaped tablespoon half-fat crème fraîche
1-2	tablespoons Cognac (or sherry)

FOR THE WORKS

2	fat cloves garlic (or 4 smaller ones), peeled
½	teaspoon Maldon sea salt
1	rounded teaspoon hot paprika
1	heaped tablespoon Delouis Fils fresh mayonnaise
6-8	French bread croûtons or bruschettine (M&S)
2	heaped tablespoons ready-grated Gruyère (Tesco and Asda)

The soup ingredients merely need to be heated together gently in a pan till hot – but not boiling. The *rouille* is made by crushing the garlic with the salt, using a pestle and mortar, till creamy, then add the paprika and pound it in. After that, add the mayonnaise and use a mini-whisk to combine it all.

the ritual: ladle the soup into warm bowls, add a dollop of *rouille* to each one and stir it in. Float croûtons or bruschettine on top, sprinkled with Gruyère, then sink them down into the liquid with your spoon and go for it, adding the rest of the croûtons or bruschettine as you do so.

serves 2-3, or 4 as a starter.

sizzling scallops with garlic butter crumbs.

This recipe is served by Nigel and Carol who own our local pub, The Swan in Monks Eleigh – a haven serving good food and wine when we're too tired to cook. The good news for cheats is that the scallops will cook beautifully from frozen (as will shelled frozen mussels if you want to ring the changes).

200g	frozen roeless scallops
2	cloves garlic, peeled
75g	soft butter
	small handful fresh parsley leaves
1	heaped tablespoon dried breadcrumbs (Waitrose Cooks' Ingredients) or dried ciabatta breadcrumbs (Tesco Ingredients)
1	tablespoon olive oil
TO SERVE	
1	dessertspoon fresh chopped parsley
2	lemon wedges

You first need to pre-heat the grill for at least 10 minutes to its highest setting. Meanwhile, place the garlic, butter, parsley and breadcrumbs in a mini-chopper, with some salt, and whiz to a paste. Then arrange the frozen scallops in 2 heat-proof, gratin dishes, preferably about 10cm in diameter, brush the oil over them and season them.

Then place the dishes about 10cm from the heat. After 4 minutes, dot the butter mixture in small pieces all over the scallops and continue cooking for about 3 minutes. At that point, stir the scallops round in the melted butter and cook for another 3-4 minutes or till the scallops are opaque in the centre (cut one open to check), the breadcrumbs are golden-brown and the butter sizzling. Sprinkle with the extra dessertspoon of parsley and serve with lemon wedges – needless to say, sizzling butter mingled with scallop juices needs masses of crusty bread (which is almost the best bit).

serves 2.

stewed beans with tomatoes & chorizo.

In Spain butter beans are called Judion beans (see photograph) – big, fat and luscious and a tapas bar regular. Since we can now buy the Greek version, called gigantes, cooked in virgin olive oil, tomatoes and herbs, we won't worry about them not being authentically Spanish for this lovely cheats' tapas, where the fragrant oil from the chorizo enhances the sauce splendidly.

355g	jar **Odysea gigantes beans in tomato sauce**
	about 10cm chorizo sausage, sliced
1	**small red onion, peeled, halved and thinly sliced**
1	**fat clove garlic, peeled and sliced**
2	**tablespoons red (or white) wine**

Heat a small saucepan over a medium heat and, when it's hot, add the slices of chorizo. Stir them around for a couple of minutes till the oil begins to seep out, then add the onion. Give that a good stir and let it cook – with the heat turned down a little – for about 5 minutes.

Then add the garlic and let it cook for 1 minute before adding the contents of the jar of beans. Rinse the jar out with the wine and add that, then turn the heat down to a gentle simmer, sprinkle in some seasoning and cook for 15 minutes without a lid.

serves 4 as part of a tapas selection.

scallops in the shell.

Here you can go for fresh plump scallops with corals (halved if they are too big) or else use the smaller queen scallops straight from the freezer. Cook them either in scallop shells, small gratin dishes or in one large dish.

225g	fresh scallops or frozen small roeless scallops
275ml	dry vermouth
1	tub (300g or 350g) fresh cheese sauce
25g	butter
2	shallots, peeled and finely chopped in a mini-chopper, or 2 tablespoons frozen diced onion
110g	small, dark-gilled mushrooms, thinly sliced
50g	ready-grated Gruyère (Tesco and Asda)
4	sprigs of fresh watercress

First, place the scallops in a medium frying-pan, pour in the vermouth and add some seasoning. Poach them for 1 minute (2 if they're frozen) or until they turn opaque. Now strain them in a sieve set over a bowl to catch the liquid, then tip the liquid back into the pan and let it bubble over a high heat and reduce until you have roughly 2 tablespoons left.

After that, pre-heat the grill to its highest setting. Then open the tub of cheese sauce and add the scallop liquid, whisking it in gently with a fork. Now, wipe the pan out with some kitchen paper, return it to the heat and melt the butter in it. Add the shallots or onion and mushrooms and cook gently for about 10 minutes, stirring now and then.

Now all you do is divide the mushroom mixture among 4 scallop shells or gratin dishes or 1 large dish, and do the same with the scallops. Then wipe out the pan with kitchen paper again, pour in the cheese sauce and gently heat it for 3 minutes. Pour this on to the scallops, followed by the grated Gruyère. Whack them under the grill about 10cm from the heat source for 3-4 minutes or until they're golden-brown on top and the sauce is bubbling. Add some freshly milled black pepper and serve, garnished with the sprigs of fresh watercress.

serves 2, or 4 as a starter.

gambas de queso.
prawns & peppers with melted Manchego cheese.

Odysea peppers in a jar are large and therefore ideal for this recipe, but others can be used if you just arrange the smaller pieces together.

150g	large cooked peeled prawns
4	pieces Odysea or Karyatis roasted red peppers, drained and sliced (or the equivalent of 1 large pepper)
110g	Manchego cheese
1	piece of jalapeño pepper, from a jar
2	cloves garlic, peeled
1	dessertspoon lemon juice
1	teaspoon olive oil

Begin by pre-heating the grill to its highest setting for about 10 minutes, then chop the jalapeño pepper and the garlic together with the lemon juice and oil in a mini-chopper. Then toss the prawns in this mixture in a bowl and add some seasoning. Next, arrange the slices of red pepper in a shallow, heatproof dish and pile the prawns in on top.

Now cut the cheese into cubes, then whiz it in the mini-chopper to 'grate' it and sprinkle it over the prawns. The whole thing now goes under the grill (10cm from the heat) until the cheese is melted and bubbling and beginning to turn golden on top – about 5 minutes.

serves 2 as a starter or part of a tapas selection.

pamboli.
Spanish tomato bread.

We always eat tons of this when we are in Majorca – so simple but so sublime! It would be good to have some gutsy country bread for this, but it's still great with a bog-standard loaf, such as a seeded bloomer.

3	large red ripe tomatoes
6	thick slices of crusty bread, cut in half
3	fat cloves garlic, peeled
1	tablespoon olive oil
6	fresh basil leaves
	Maldon sea salt

First, for the tomatoes: skin them (1 minute in boiling water from the kettle and the skins will slip off easily), then cut into quarters. Place them in a mini-chopper, together with the garlic cloves, olive oil and some seasoning, and simply whiz to a purée. Now empty this into a sieve set over a bowl and let the excess liquid drain off for about 5 minutes.

Meanwhile, toast the bread lightly on one side, then spread the tomato pulp on to the untoasted side. Sprinkle with sea salt, freshly milled black pepper and a basil leaf on each slice.

note: this can be made more substantial – as in Spain – by topping it with Ibérico ham or thin slices of chorizo.

serves 6 as part of a tapas selection.

73

lazy lunch.

Roquefort & leek tart

asparagus with no-panic Hollandaise

cool!

as in summer.

for an up-to-date ingredients list go to www.deliaonline.com

asparagus with no-panic Hollandaise.

One of the nicest summer dishes of all. To make it more substantial, you could add a couple of poached eggs. This is an inauthentic version of Hollandaise without all the panic of curdling butter and with less fat. I've watched people tasting this and not noticing it isn't the real thing

600g fresh asparagus

FOR THE NO-PANIC HOLLANDAISE

3	rounded tablespoons crème fraîche
1	teaspoon cornflour
2	egg yolks
¾	tablespoon white wine vinegar (Tesco Finest Chardonnay white wine vinegar is good) or white balsamic vinegar
½	tablespoon lemon juice
2	tablespoons (50g) softened butter

To prepare the asparagus, snap off the woody ends (just bend each stalk and the bit that snaps off is the bit you don't want). By far the best way to cook asparagus is in a fan steamer placed in a frying-pan with a lid: to do this, add boiling water from the kettle to the pan to a depth of about 2.5cm. Place the stalks on the spread-out steamer and sit the steamer in the pan. Add some salt, and simmer with the lid on for 4-6 minutes.

Spoon the crème fraîche into a small saucepan, then add the rest of the ingredients except for the butter. Whisk them all together with a mini whisk, then, over a medium heat, bring the whole lot up to simmering point, whisking continuously, until the sauce has thickened. Now, remove the sauce from the heat, taste and add more seasoning, vinegar or lemon if required, then whisk in the butter – and that's it. Serve the asparagus on hot plates with ground pepper and the sauce poured over (you'll also need good bread to mop up the juices!).

note: you can make the Hollandaise sauce in advance and re-heat it, set over a pan of hot water.

serves 4 as a starter.

salmorejo. chilled Spanish soup.

This was a very enthusiastic shot in the dark after we returned from a brilliant holiday travelling through Spain. Our waiter in Spain was emphatic: it had to be much thicker than gazpacho, well chilled and garnished with chopped, hardboiled egg and snippets of Ibérico ham. We got it, and here it is. Perfect if the weather is really hot.

300g	pack large ripe vine tomatoes
2	large (about 200g) red peppers, preferably Romano, de-seeded and roughly chopped
75g	dried breadcrumbs (Waitrose Cooks' Ingredients) or dried ciabatta breadcrumbs (Tesco Ingredients)
110ml	extra virgin olive oil, preferably Spanish
3	cloves garlic, peeled
1	tablespoon Spanish sherry vinegar (Sainsbury's)

FOR THE GARNISH

1	hardboiled egg, peeled and chopped in a mini-chopper
2	slices Jambon Ibérico ham, cut into small strips

The only real work here is to pour boiling water on to the tomatoes, wait 1 minute then drain them and slip the skins off.

Now place the tomatoes and all the rest of the ingredients into a sturdy bowl and season. Begin with your stick blender on low and whiz to a thick creamy purée. Then cover the bowl with clingfilm and chill overnight – or for as long as possible. To serve, chill the soup bowls, and in spite of our waiter you don't *have* to have the garnishes (but they are nice).

serves 2, or 4 as a starter.

Spanish tuna salad with peppers, olives & artichokes.

This recipe comes from Liceras, a region of Spain where Pauline, our recipe tester, has a house. This is her version of a very popular local salad that's served throughout the region.

220g   jar best-quality Spanish tuna, drained (Ortiz is good)
275g   Odysea or Karyatis roasted red peppers, drained and chopped
75g   pitted black Kalamata olives (Sainsbury's or other)
280g   jar chargrilled artichoke hearts, drained and halved
150g   crispy leaf salad
50g   rocket leaves
540g   jar large Judion beans (El Artesano from Sainsbury's are good) or regular butter beans, drained and rinsed
240g   pack Sunblush tomatoes (Sainsbury's Taste the Difference), drained
75g   seedless white grapes

FOR THE DRESSING
2   tablespoons extra virgin olive oil
1   tablespoon Spanish sherry vinegar (Sainsbury's)
       grated zest of 1 lemon
       juice of ½ lemon

Start by whisking the dressing ingredients together. Then mix the crispy leaf salad with the rocket and arrange about one-third on a large serving plate. Layer up with the beans, peppers, Sunblush tomatoes, tuna and artichokes and the rest of the leaves, seasoning as you go. Scatter the grapes and olives on top, then finally drizzle the dressing over. Serve immediately with, I would suggest, some Spanish tomato bread (pamboli) – see page 73.

serves 4.

avocado with prawns 2 ways.

There are some quite ordinary yet lovely things that end up being overlooked because they are not fashionable, and this is one of them – avocado with prawns. We've made it with Tesco Finest prawn cocktail here, but any similar one is fine.

200g	prawn cocktail (Tesco Finest)
	cayenne pepper
1	fresh lime
2	heaped tablespoons Whole Earth organic tomato ketchup
1	large, ripe avocado
	shredded lettuce (if using)
	traditional Irish wheaten loaf (Tesco), cut into thinnish slices and buttered

First, empty the prawn cocktail into a bowl, add some seasoning and a good pinch of cayenne. Now add the juice of half the lime along with the ketchup, and stir it all together.

Pile the mixture into the halved avocado. Alternatively, cut the avocado into chunks and pile this, along with the prawn cocktail, on top of some shredded lettuce in 2 glasses to serve. Either way, add a sprinkling of cayenne, the other half of the lime cut into quarters to squeeze over and serve with some of the lovely Irish bread alongside.

serves 2.

lazy summer soup.

You have two options here: one is to chill the soup thoroughly and serve in ice-cold bowls, which will be wonderfully refreshing if the weather is hot. Or if global warming is still on hold, serve it hot. Either way, garnish it with extra watercress leaves just before serving.

about 10 discs Aunt Bessie's Homestyle frozen mashed potato
110g   watercress, spinach and rocket salad
1   medium leek, trimmed, washed and sliced
4   thick spring onions, or 6 medium ones, snipped into three pieces
425ml hot stock made from Marigold bouillon powder
150ml milk
1   teaspoon butter
extra watercress leaves, to serve

In a medium saucepan melt the butter, then add the sliced leek and spring onions. Stir them around, add some salt, put the lid on and cook gently for 5 minutes. After that, add the frozen potato, stock and milk and bring everything up to simmering point.

Give it one good stir, cover the pan and simmer gently for 20 minutes. Then, off the heat, add the watercress, spinach and rocket leaves, then gently whiz the soup to a purée with a stick blender – though not too much, you still need to see bits of leaves. Taste and check the seasoning before serving, garnished with the extra watercress.

serves 2-3, or 4 as a starter.

uncool
what mums used to make.

for an up-to-date ingredients list go to www.deliaonline.com

bangers with caramelised red onions & mustard mash.

Everyone loves bangers and mash and now we don't have to peel, boil or mash the potatoes it's great to enjoy it a bit more often.

400g pack of 6 Suffolk recipe pork sausages (Co-op)
      or other good-quality pork sausages (see page 248 for stockists)
100g (half a 200g jar) English Provender very lazy caramelised
      red onions
1   dessertspoon olive oil
150ml red wine
1   tablespoon red wine vinegar (Tesco Finest Chianti red wine
      vinegar is good)
1   heaped teaspoon fresh thyme leaves
FOR THE MUSTARD MASH
1   tablespoon grain mustard (Tiptree organic hot English is good)
      about 10 discs Aunt Bessie's Homestyle frozen mashed potato
1   dessertspoon half-fat crème fraîche
      knob of butter

Heat the oil in a frying-pan and fry the sausages over a medium heat, turning them once or twice, for 15-20 minutes. After that, turn the heat up, pour in the red wine, red wine vinegar and add the thyme and let it bubble and reduce for 1 minute before adding the caramelised red onions. Stir them around to melt and cook on a low heat for about 2 minutes, then add some seasoning.

Cook the mashed potato from frozen according to the instructions on the pack, then beat in the rest of the ingredients and some seasoning. Serve with the sausages, with the sauce poured over.

serves 2.

steak & kidney easy.

This recipe may sound a bit unlikely, but while I would not claim it is quite the traditional version, it runs it pretty close. Trust me.

400g	tin steak and kidney (M&S)
375g	pack Jus-Rol fresh ready-rolled shortcrust pastry sheet
1	medium onion, peeled
1	dessertspoon groundnut or other flavourless oil
¼	teaspoon gravy browning
1	dessertspoon Worcestershire sauce
	a little flour, for rolling out
1	medium egg, beaten

Firstly, don't make the same mistake I made. Follow the instructions on the pastry pack and remove it from the fridge 40 minutes before you need it, other-wise it cracks as you unroll it. Also, pre-heat the oven to gas mark 7, 220°C.

To start with, halve and thinly slice the onion. Heat the oil, then fry the onion until it's quite brown and softened, which will take about 10 minutes. Then remove it from the heat and allow it to cool. Next, empty the steak and kidney into a bowl (at which stage you will see why I've included gravy browning to give a good rich colour), stir in the gravy browning and Worcestershire sauce, then add a little salt and a generous amount of freshly milled black pepper.

Now, unfold the pastry on to a floured board and roll it out until it's about 2.5cm larger all round, then transfer it to a large, well-greased baking sheet. Add the cooked onion to the meat, mix together and arrange over one half of the pastry, leaving a 2.5cm border. Then brush the border with some of the beaten egg and fold the other half of the pastry over. Seal it well, trim the edges then fold them inwards and either make an imprint all round with your thumb, or a fork.

Lastly, brush the whole lot with beaten egg, make a steam hole about the size of a ten-pence piece in the centre and bake on a high shelf for 25-30 minutes.

serves 2-3.

my mum's macaroni cheese.

No, she didn't cheat, but she always put other things in her macaroni cheese, like bacon and mushrooms and tomatoes on top. With or without additions, it has to be the ultimate comfort food.

225g	Martelli maccheroni (or any other good-quality dried pasta)
2	tubs (each 300g) fresh ready-prepared three-cheese sauce (Sainsbury's)
250g	ready-grated mature Cheddar
	olive oil
4	rashers smoked back bacon, chopped not too small
1	medium onion, peeled, quartered and chopped in a mini chopper, or 3 tablespoons frozen diced onion
75g	chestnut mushrooms, cut into chunks
1	rounded tablespoon half-fat crème fraiche
1	bunch small ripe cherry tomatoes on the vine
2	tablespoons fresh ready-grated Parmesan (for sprinkling)

Pre-heat the grill to its highest setting

First, cook the maccheroni in 2.25 litres boiling, salted water for 10-12 minutes and put a gratin dish (we used one about 18cm square) underneath the grill to heat through. Meanwhile, heat 1 dessertspoon of oil in a frying-pan, then add the chopped bacon and onion and cook for about 5 minutes on a medium heat before adding the mushrooms and cooking for a further 10 minutes.

While that's happening, heat the cheese sauce in a saucepan and when it's bubbling stir in the crème fraîche and Cheddar. When the pasta's ready, tip it first into a colander to drain off the water, then quickly back into the saucepan.

Next, add the contents of the frying-pan to the pasta, followed by the cheese sauce (as fast as you can so as not to lose the heat). Add a good grinding of black pepper and a little salt, stir well, then transfer the whole lot to the heated gratin dish. Now snip the bunch of tomatoes in half and place them on top, drizzle a little oil over each tomato, then sprinkle the Parmesan all over. Place the dish under the grill (10cm from the heat) for 5-7 minutes, or until the cheese and sauce are golden-brown and bubbling and the tomatoes have softened.

serves 4.

good old shepherd's pie.

You won't believe this one until you try it – nothing short of sensational, I would say. Everybody loves shepherd's pie, but few have the time to make it... until now!

400g	tin minced lamb (M&S)
1	largish onion, peeled, quartered and chopped in a mini chopper, or 4 tablespoons frozen diced onion
175g	ready-prepared diced mixed carrot and swede (Tesco)
1	dessertspoon olive oil
1	teaspoon fresh thyme
½	teaspoon ground cinnamon

FOR THE TOPPING

	about 16 discs Aunt Bessie's Homestyle frozen mashed potato
2	medium leeks, trimmed (use the white parts only)
3	heaped tablespoons ready-grated mature Cheddar

Pre-heat the oven to gas mark 6, 200°C. Start by heating the oil in a largish frying-pan till very hot, add the onion, carrot and swede and cook them for about 5 minutes, keeping the heat high, to colour a bit at the edges, stirring them around.

After that, combine the vegetables with the minced lamb, thyme, cinnamon and some seasoning and transfer the whole lot to an 18cm square baking dish (or similar). Next, arrange the potato discs on top, slightly overlapping. The leeks should be cut vertically to halfway down and fanned out under cold, running water to remove any dirt, then sliced through to the bottom, then across very finely. Sprinkle the leeks all over the potato, followed by the grated Cheddar. Then put it into the oven for 35-40 minutes, till the top is crusty and golden.

Let it settle for about 10 minutes before serving – a bag of ready-shredded spring greens would go down a treat with this.

note: for cottage pie, a 400g tin of M&S minced beef is every bit as good. If you use ready-prepared swede and carrot from elsewhere, it may be in larger chunks, which need to be chopped a bit smaller in the mini-chopper.

serves 4.

thick pea & bacon soup.

This truly is like mum used to make – without the overnight soaking and long simmering. It's also very nutritious and very cheap, and takes about 20 minutes from start to finish. The spring onions and green leaves add a freshness to this, but in winter spinach leaves would be good.

538g	**tin (or 2 x 300g tins) marrowfat peas**
1	**pack (about 50g) ready-cooked crispy smoked bacon**
1	**teaspoon butter**
4	**thick spring onions, including the green parts, chopped into 3 or 4 pieces**
	the outside leaves of 1 lettuce
2 ½	**teaspoons Marigold bouillon powder**

Begin by draining the peas in a large sieve or colander and rinsing them under the cold tap, reserving the tin. Then, in a medium saucepan, melt the butter, add the spring onions along with the lettuce leaves. Add a little salt, put a lid on and let them sweat gently for 5 minutes.

After that, add the peas and half the crispy bacon (which will crumble into bits easily in your hands). Fill the empty pea tin with boiling water, whisk in the bouillon (stock) powder, then – holding the tin with a cloth – add the stock to the saucepan. Replace the lid and simmer gently for 10 minutes. Next, using a stick blender, whiz to a purée in the pan. Taste and season before ladling the soup into warmed bowls, then add the rest of the bacon, crumbled as before.

serves 2, or 4 as a starter.

amazing moussaka.

It's amazing in that authentic moussaka is quite a long, drawn-out affair, whilst this one is made in half the time.

400g	tin minced lamb (M&S)
250g	tub ricotta cheese
1	tub (300g or 350g) ready-prepared fresh cheese sauce
2	tablespoons red wine
2	tablespoons sun-dried tomato paste
1	teaspoon ground cinnamon
1	tablespoon chopped fresh mint
2	eggs
	whole nutmeg, for grating
3-4	frozen chargrilled aubergine slices (Asda)
1	tablespoon fresh ready-grated Parmesan

Pre-heat the oven to gas mark 4, 180°C. First of all, mix the red wine, tomato paste, cinnamon and mint together in a bowl, then add the contents of the tin of lamb. Mix all of this together thoroughly, adding some seasoning.

Next, the topping: all you do here is whisk the ricotta cheese and the cheese sauce together, then beat the eggs and add them to the sauce with some seasoning and a few good gratings of nutmeg, then whisk again.

Now, in a baking dish (19cm square, or similar), spread the meat mixture over the base. Then, using scissors, snip the frozen aubergine slices into three and arrange them over the meat. Finish off with the ricotta sauce. Finally, sprinkle the Parmesan over the surface and bake on a high shelf in the oven for 50 minutes-1 hour or until the top is golden-brown. This goes nicely with rice and a Greek salad (see page 152).

serves 4.

memories of goulash.

This was so popular in the '60s (I still cherish fond memories of it) and lends itself easily to cheating. Instead of a green pepper, you can use half a jar of M&S roasted red and yellow peppers (well drained) if that suits.

800g	diced braising steak
1	large onion, peeled
1	large green pepper, halved and de-seeded
1	clove garlic, peeled and crushed
1	tablespoon plain flour
1	dessertspoon hot paprika
1	dessertspoon La Chinata or El Avion sweet smoked paprika, plus a little extra for sprinkling
2	jars (each 300g) Heinz tomato frito

150ml red wine
150ml soured cream

Pre-heat the oven to gas mark 1, 140°C. What you need to do is chop the onion roughly into largish chunks, and the same with the pepper, then place them in a bowl with the crushed garlic.

Then add the cubes of meat, the flour, both types of paprika and some seasoning. Now mix everything together with your hands so it all gets a good coating of flour and paprika, then tip the whole lot into a medium, flameproof casserole. Next, mix the tomato frito with the wine, then pour that over the rest of the ingredients, give it all a good stir and bring it up to a gentle simmer on top of the stove.

Cover with a tight lid, then pop it into the oven and leave to cook for 3 hours. To serve, add the soured cream – but don't mix it in, what you need is a sort of marbling effect – and sprinkle on a little more smoked paprika. We like this served with brown rice (Waitrose frozen is good).

serves 4.

banana bread pudding with toffee sauce.

This is a lightened-up version of the old English classic that used leftover bread. Cheats just need to grab some dried breadcrumbs (or Waitrose does Mr Crumb fresh breadcrumbs – for stuffing) and throw it all together. Serve it hot for a pudding and, if there's any left over, it's great cold as well. Thick cream or vanilla ice cream is also a must.

FOR THE BANANA BREAD PUDDING

2	medium bananas, peeled and roughly chopped
110g	dried breadcrumbs (Waitrose Cooks' Ingredients) or dried ciabatta breadrumbs (Tesco Ingredients)
150ml	milk
25g	melted butter, plus a little extra for greasing
1	rounded teaspoon ground mixed spice
50g	dark muscovado sugar
50g	mixed dried fruit
1	egg, beaten

FOR THE TOPPING AND TOFFEE SAUCE

1	tablespoon unrefined demerara sugar
1	teaspoon ground cinnamon
320g	jar rich caramel toffee sauce (M&S)

As it says above, just throw all the banana bread pudding ingredients into a bowl, give them a really good mix and leave to soak for about 30 minutes while you pre-heat the oven to gas mark 4, 180°C.

Then, pack the mixture into a buttered 15cm square baking dish. For the topping, mix the demerara sugar and cinnamon, then sprinkle that all over the top. Bake the pudding on the centre shelf of the oven for 35-45 minutes. Serve it cut into squares, with the rich caramel sauce, gently warmed, poured over.

serves 4.

easy as apple pie.

If you are one of those people who can never resist a slice of real home-made apple pie with a freshly baked, very crisp, melt-in-the-mouth crust and a pile of fluffy, fragrant, clove-scented apples inside – here it is!

700g	mixed Cox's and Bramley apples
230g	Jus-Rol fresh large shortcrust pastry case
1	heaped tablespoon golden caster sugar
6	whole cloves
1	egg white, lightly whisked
200g	Jus-Rol fresh shortcrust pie lid, 24cm in diameter
1	tablespoon unrefined demerara sugar

Pre-heat the oven to gas mark 6, 200°C. First, place the pastry case, still in its foil container, on a baking sheet. Then, all you do is halve, core and slice the apples (I leave the skins on) and pile them into the pastry case (making them higher in the centre), sprinkle over the caster sugar and dot with the cloves. Next, dampen the edges with some of the egg white and place the pastry lid over the apples. Seal the edges, crimping all round with your thumb or a fork.

Make a steam hole in the centre about the size of a 50p-piece, then brush the pastry all over with the beaten egg white, and sprinkle the demerara sugar over that. Now pop it into the centre of the oven to bake for 30-40 minutes, until the apples are cooked and tender when tested with a skewer. Serve with thick cream, custard or ice-cream.

serves 4-6.

food for friends.

Caribbean chicken with salsa.

chicken on
the run

real quick.

Caribbean chicken with salsa.

A dead simple recipe this, with a wonderfully exotic combination of textures and flavours. Perfect for serving to friends.

4	chicken thighs and 4 drumsticks
1	heaped dessertspoon English Provender very lazy ginger
1	rounded dessertspoon ground ginger
2	rounded tablespoons dark muscovado sugar
2	cloves garlic, peeled
	grated zest and juice of 2 limes

FOR THE SALSA

400g	ready-prepared fresh mango chunks
2	pieces jalapeño pepper, from a jar
2	pieces roasted red and yellow peppers from a jar (M&S)
1	small red onion, peeled and quartered
	zest and juice of 1 lime
half a	400g tin Epicure black beans, rinsed and drained
	small handful fresh coriander leaves

Pre-heat the oven to gas mark 7, 220°C. Start this by whizzing the ginger, ground ginger, sugar, garlic, lime zest and juice in a mini-chopper to make a paste. Next, make 2 diagonal cuts in each chicken thigh and drumstick and spread the paste all over. Now place the chicken in an ovenproof dish or a small roasting tin and bake it on a high shelf for 40-45 minutes or until cooked through.

Meanwhile, empty all the salsa ingredients except for the black beans and coriander into a bowl, then transfer half to the mini-chopper. Chop them, not too small, then repeat with the other half. Mix with the beans and the coriander leaves in a bowl. Serve the chicken with the salsa handed round separately.

note: the rest of the black beans could be heated and mixed with cooked rice to serve with the chicken, or else used to make a half-quantity of the Black Bean & Jalapeño Dip on page 173.

serves 4.

chicken on the run

a sort of chicken Basque.

The original version of this was one of the most popular recipes I've ever published, because no accompaniment was needed and it was all cooked in one pot. So welcome to the cheat's version: same again, only quicker, and a perfect supper dish for two.

2	chicken breasts, skin on, preferably part-boned
1-2	dessertspoons olive oil
1	medium onion, peeled
1	clove garlic, peeled
75g	chorizo sausage (in one piece)
150ml	Spanish Calasparra or Italian carnaroli rice
275ml	dry white wine
300ml	jar Heinz tomato frito
half a	285g jar roasted red and yellow peppers (M&S), drained
1	teaspoon La Chinata or El Avion sweet smoked Spanish paprika
1	tablespoon pitted black Kalamata olives (Sainsbury's or other)

First, put a dessertspoon of oil in a medium flameproof casserole and, when it is shimmering hot, season the chicken breasts and brown them in the hot oil on both sides. While this is happening, cut the onion in half and then into thick slices. Cut the garlic into thin slices and cut the chorizo into 1cm slices, or small cubes if you bought a chunky one.

When the chicken is golden-brown on both sides, remove it to a plate using a slotted spoon. Then, add the onion, garlic and chorizo to the hot pan and toss these around. If you want to, add a spot more oil (the onion needs to be tinged brown around the edges).

After that, stir in the rice, followed by the wine, the tomato frito, the peppers and the smoked paprika and, as soon as it comes up to simmering point, replace the chicken breasts and scatter in the olives. Add some seasoning, put the lid on and turn the heat to its lowest setting, then let it cook very gently without disturbing it for 30-35 minutes.

serves 2.

chicken tonnato.

If you live in the sticks like we do, a joint of veal for the classic version of this dish is not an option. However, this wonderful sauce also goes very well with chicken – lovely for an alfresco summer lunch.

2	ready-cooked chicken breasts
50g	best-quality tuna fish from a tin or jar
150ml	Delouis Fils fresh mayonnaise
3	tinned anchovy fillets in extra virgin olive oil (Sainsbury's), drained
1½	tablespoons capers, rinsed and drained
1	teaspoon lemon juice (or more, to taste)
	lemon slices, to serve

For the sauce, put the mayonnaise in a mini-chopper. Then drain the tuna and add that, along with 1 of the anchovy fillets and 1 tablespoon of the capers. Now whiz everything together till smooth, add 3 tablespoons of cold water and whiz again. Next, do a bit of tasting and season with the lemon juice and some freshly milled black pepper.

Now, remove the skin from the chicken breasts and slice them very thinly lengthways. Arrange the slices in a shallow serving dish, then spoon the sauce over. Garnish with the remaining anchovy fillets, split lengthways and arranged in a zig-zag pattern on top of the sauce, scatter over the remaining capers and serve with lemon slices.

serves 2.

chicken & leek pot pie.

An unlikely sounding combination perhaps but, trust me, it is really very good.

400g	tin chunky chicken in white sauce (M&S)
1	medium leek, trimmed and thinly sliced
1	teaspoon butter
1	small carrot, peeled and very thinly sliced
2	tablespoons dry vermouth
1	tablespoon half-fat crème fraîche
1	teaspoon chopped fresh tarragon
2	Jus-Rol frozen small individual puff pastry rounds, defrosted for about 15 minutes (covered with a cloth)
1	medium egg, beaten

Pre-heat the oven to gas mark 6, 200°C. Begin by melting the butter in a small saucepan, then stir in the leek and carrot and let them soften over a medium heat for 5 minutes. Then add the vermouth, cover the pan and cook for a further minute. Empty the contents of the tin of chicken into a bowl, season, then stir in the crème fraîche and tarragon, followed by the leek and carrot.

Spoon all this into a small oval pie dish (about 18cm long and 5cm deep) and dampen the edge of the dish. Next, cut the pastry rounds in half and arrange the halves, overlapping each other, over the pie. Press the pastry down well all round the edge and trim off any overhanging bits with a knife. Now brush the pastry with beaten egg and bake the pie for 20 minutes, then turn the heat down to gas mark 4, 180°C and bake for a further 10 minutes till crisp and golden-brown. Serve with a leafy, green vegetable such as spinach.

serves 2.

Mexican chicken chilli with cheese.

Mexican? That might be stretching it a bit, but the original idea did come from there, and I know you'll love it.

2	largish skinless chicken breasts
2	pieces jalapeño pepper, from a jar
75g	ready-grated mozzarella
1	small green pepper, de-seeded and roughly chopped
1	medium onion, peeled and quartered
2	cloves garlic, peeled
1	teaspoon cumin seeds
1	tablespoon groundnut or other flavourless oil
1	rounded tablespoon plain flour
425ml	hot stock made from Marigold bouillon powder
410g	tin Tarantella organic pinto beans (Co-op) or borlotti beans
2	tablespoons fresh coriander leaves
1	fresh lime, quartered

The preparation will take about 10 minutes: all you do is cut the chicken into smallish, bite-size chunks. Next, use a mini-chopper to chop the green pepper, onion, garlic and jalapeño – use the pulse button so as not to let it get too fine.

Now crush the cumin seeds with a pestle and mortar (or the back of a table-spoon on a flat surface). Heat a medium shallow pan, add the crushed cumin seeds and let them toast a bit to draw out their flavour. Then add the oil and, when it's sizzling, add the pepper and onion mixture. Cook these, tossing them around the pan, for about 5 minutes or until they take on some colour. Then stir in the flour and, once it has soaked in, add the stock – stirring the whole time – then add the chicken and the beans (the latter need to be drained, then rinsed well under cold running water first).

Now add some salt, put a lid on and let the whole lot simmer gently for 20 minutes, then add the grated mozzarella. Stir well and let it simmer (this time without a lid) for a further 15 minutes. Finally, just before serving, add the coriander leaves and stir them in. Serve with rice or tortillas and lime quarters to squeeze over.

serves 2-3.

120

spiced chicken masala with coconut sambal.

Another very quick curry using ready-blended spices. If you like the sambal, stock up with the coconut as it freezes really well.

2	chicken breasts, skin on
4	teaspoons Seasoned Pioneers tandoori masala spice blend
2	teaspoons groundnut or other flavourless oil
2	cloves garlic, peeled
1	medium onion, peeled and quartered
1	teaspoon English Provender very lazy ginger
200ml	tub half-fat crème fraîche

FOR THE COCONUT SAMBAL

50g	fresh organic coconut chunks (Waitrose)
½	small onion, peeled
1	tablespoon lime juice
½	piece jalapeño pepper, from a jar
½	teaspoon salt

To make the sambal, simply add all the ingredients to a mini-chopper and whiz until everything is very finely chopped (you will need to stop to push the ingredients down into the chopper occasionally).

Heat 1 teaspoon of the oil in a medium saucepan until very hot. Cut the chicken into largish pieces and brown half of them in the hot oil, tossing them around till golden-brown all over. Then remove them to a plate and brown the other half.

Meanwhile, finely chop the garlic, onion and ginger in a mini-chopper. When all the chicken has been browned and removed from the pan, add the rest of the oil and cook the chopped mixture for about 5 minutes, or till tinged brown at the edges. Next, add the tandoori masala spice blend, stir that around for a few seconds, then return the chicken to the saucepan. Add some seasoning and stir in the crème fraîche. Bring to a simmer and cook gently, with the lid on, for 10-15 minutes. Serve with the coconut sambal.

serves 2.

Moroccan chicken with preserved lemon & chickpeas.

Just imagine having to shop for galangal, rose petals, ginger, cinnamon, allspice, cardamom, cassia, coriander, mace, nutmeg and cloves. Well, hurray, you don't have to because this all comes dry-roasted and blended from Seasoned Pioneers to bring, as they say, `the authentic taste of Morocco to your kitchen´.

2	chicken thighs and 2 drumsticks
2	Belazu preserved lemons, quartered
100g	frozen cooked chickpeas (Tesco Whole Foods), defrosted for 10 minutes at room temperature
2	dessertspoons olive oil
1	fairly large red onion, peeled, halved and thinly sliced
1	tablespoon Seasoned Pioneers Ras-el-Hanout spice blend
2	fat cloves garlic, peeled and sliced
6-8	green olives
275ml	dry white wine
	fresh coriander leaves, to finish

First of all, heat 1 dessertspoon of the oil in a medium flameproof casserole and, when it's hot, stir in the onion and let it cook over a high heat for about 5 minutes. Meanwhile, mix half the spice blend with the other dessertspoon of olive oil and, after making cuts into the flesh of the chicken with a sharp knife, rub the oil-and-spice mixture all over the surface and into the cuts.

Now stir the garlic and the rest of the spice mix into the onions, add the lemon quarters, olives and chickpeas and place the chicken joints on top. Pour in the wine, season with salt and, when it reaches simmering point, cover the casserole, turn the heat down to its lowest setting and cook for 1 hour. Serve sprinkled with coriander. This is good served with rice or couscous and maybe a salad.

serves 2.

shortcut chicken cacciatora.

Whilst the partnership of tomato with basil usually gets top billing on the culinary scene, it's our opinion that tomatoes with rosemary are equally good. As are tomatoes and sage...but that's another story.

8	plump chicken thighs
300g	jar Heinz tomato frito
1	tablespoon olive oil
1	medium onion, peeled and quartered
2	cloves garlic, peeled
1	dessertspoon fresh rosemary, plus 4 small sprigs
175ml	dry white wine
2	tablespoons white wine vinegar (Tesco Finest Chardonnay white wine vinegar is good)

First, in a medium flameproof casserole, heat the oil and, when it's hot, season the chicken thighs and sauté them on all sides till golden. While that's happening, chop the onion, garlic and the dessertspoon of rosemary in a mini-chopper – using a pulse action so they're not too finely chopped.

When the chicken is golden, remove it to a plate with a slotted spoon or tongs, then add the onion mixture to the pan and sauté it for about 5-6 minutes – stirring it around now and then – till softened. Now return the chicken thighs to the pan, pour in the tomato frito, then rinse out the jar with the white wine and wine vinegar and add that too, along with the sprigs of rosemary. Give it all a good stir to combine everything, add some seasoning, then bring to the boil before turning the heat down to its lowest setting, cover and leave to barely simmer for about 40 minutes.

This is great served with egg pasta (such as green tagliatelle) or tiny new potatoes and a green leafy salad. Oh, and of course the rest of your white wine!

serves 4.

asian express
Oriental gravy training.

Vietnamese beef patties.

Supper for two? Go to the Far East, or at least bring it into your kitchen with these brilliant little patties. It has to be said they also work just as well with minced pork or lamb.

225g	minced beef
½	red onion, peeled
50g	sachet Patak's creamed coconut
1	rounded tablespoon Whole Earth crunchy organic peanut butter
1	dessertspoon Thai fish sauce
1	teaspoon ground cumin
½	teaspoon soft brown sugar

FOR THE PEANUT DIPPING SAUCE

2	tablespoons Kikkoman soy sauce
2	tablespoons Whole Earth crunchy organic peanut butter
2	pieces jalapeño pepper, from a jar
2	tablespoons Whole Earth organic tomato ketchup
2	cloves garlic, peeled and crushed
	juice of 1 small lime
1	tablespoon chopped, roasted peanuts

Pre-heat the grill to its highest setting for 10 minutes. Chop the onion and creamed coconut together in a mini-chopper, then scrape the mixture out into a bowl containing the beef and the rest of the patty ingredients. Mix everything really well, then, using your hands, shape it into 12 small, round patties.

For the dipping sauce, put all the ingredients (except for the chopped peanuts) in a mini-chopper with 2 tablespoons water, then whiz to a purée. Pour into a bowl and garnish with the chopped, roasted peanuts.

To cook the patties, place them on the grill rack under a hot grill, 10cm from the heat, and grill for 3 minutes on each side. Serve them with the bowl of Peanut Dipping Sauce to dunk into.

serves 2.

Vietnamese spring rolls with dipping sauce.

The real cheat element here is that it's mega-fast to prepare but looks as though it took an age!

8	Blue Dragon Vietnamese spring roll wrappers
24	large cooked peeled prawns, split in half lengthways
4	lettuce leaves, finely shredded
¼	cucumber, seeds removed and cut into fine strips
4	spring onions, cut into fine shreds
1	tablespoon roughly chopped roasted peanuts
2	tablespoons fresh coriander leaves

FOR THE DIPPING SAUCE

1	tablespoon Kikkoman soy sauce
	juice of 1 lime
1	tablespoon toasted sesame oil
1	dessertspoon Thai fish sauce
1	teaspoon chopped spring onion (green parts only)
1	piri piri chilli from a jar (Tesco Ingredients or Waitrose Cooks' Ingredients), stalk removed, de-seeded and finely chopped

Pour some warm water into a roasting tin, and have a clean tea-towel laid out flat on the work-surface. Put 1 spring roll wrapper into the water for 30 seconds, then remove and lay it flat on the tea-towel. Turn it over to remove any excess water. Arrange 4 prawn halves (pink side down) in the centre of the third of the wrapper nearest to you. Top with some lettuce, cucumber, spring onion, peanuts and coriander and finish off with 2 more prawn halves (pink side facing upwards).

Fold the edge of the wrapper nearest to you over the filling, and bring the edges over that, then tightly roll away from you right to the end to form a parcel (it is important to be firm and roll it really tight). Finally, take a sharp knife and cut the rolls in half diagonally – about 1cm in from each end. Repeat with the other spring rolls (they can be made several hours ahead; keep them covered with damp kitchen paper in the fridge). For the dipping sauce, mix the first 4 ingredients together, sprinkle with spring onions and chilli and serve with the spring rolls.

serves 4 as a starter or snack.

131

Thai green prawn curry.

If there were prizes for cheats' ingredients, this frozen Thai curry mix would win one. Anyone who has trudged around Asian shops or scanned websites knows how hard it is to find authentic Thai ingredients. Now, the whole lot comes in one pack and you can whiz it in the mini-chopper for a perfect Thai curry any time you feel like it. We've used prawns here but it also works well with cooked chicken – absolutely brilliant.

400g	frozen raw tiger or king prawns
295g	pack frozen Thai curry mix (Asda; available from end March 2008)
1	dessertspoon oil
3	tins (each 165ml) Blue Dragon light coconut milk
1	tablespoon Thai fish sauce
1	teaspoon Seasoned Pioneers Thai shrimp paste
1	teaspoon palm (or soft brown) sugar

Take the individual Thai mix ingredients from their packet and leave for 20 minutes to defrost slightly. Then, leaving the kaffir lime leaves to one side, place half of the rest of the ingredients in a mini-chopper and give them a really good blast to reduce them to a coarse paste (you will need to persevere to deal with the lemon grass). Then repeat with the other half.

Now heat the oil in a saucepan, add the curry paste and cook this over a medium heat, stirring now and then, for a couple of minutes. Next add the frozen prawns and cook for 2 minutes until pink on both sides. Then add the coconut milk and fish sauce and stir in the shrimp paste and palm sugar.

Heat everything until bubbling, then cook, uncovered, for another 5 minutes until the prawns are properly cooked through. Finally, roll up the reserved kaffir lime leaves and slice them into the thinnest possible strips, then stir them into the curry. Serve with lots of Thai jasmine rice to absorb all the lovely fragrant sauce.

serves 4.

134

sesame scallops with rice noodles.

From the freezer and storecupboard to the table in roughly 20 minutes. Not bad.

200g frozen roeless scallops
110g dried rice noodles (soaked according to instructions, then drained)
1 stalk Blue Dragon whole lemongrass (from a jar), cut into 3 pieces
1 teaspoon English Provender very lazy ginger
1 teaspoon light soft brown sugar
4 tablespoons Kikkoman soy sauce
2 tablespoons toasted sesame oil
1 tablespoon sesame seeds
75g sugar-snap peas, halved lengthways on the diagonal
2 spring onions, finely sliced diagonally

First, put the lemongrass, ginger, sugar, soy and sesame oil into a mini-chopper and chop small. Heat a large frying-pan, then add the sesame seeds and shake them now and then over the heat for about 3 minutes until they are a deep golden-brown. Then transfer them to a plate and keep on one side.

Transfer the lemongrass-and-ginger mixture to the frying-pan, add the frozen scallops, bring up to simmering point and simmer gently, uncovered, for 10 minutes or till the scallops are opaque in the centre (cut one open to check). After that, remove the cooked scallops with a slotted spoon and keep them warm whilst you add the noodles and sugar-snap peas to the pan and toss together for 2-3 minutes in the sauce. Pile on to a serving dish, top with the scallops, then the spring onions and toasted sesame seeds.

serves 2.

Asian steak sandwiches.

No not bread sarnies. These are slices of sticky, fragrant marinated steak, served wrapped in lettuce leaves.

225g trimmed rump or sirloin steak
      oil, for frying
2   spring onions, cut lengthways into shreds
10cm piece fresh cucumber, cut lengthways into matchsticks
2   tablespoons fresh coriander leaves
1   Iceberg lettuce (use the pliable leafy parts)

FOR THE MARINADE

2   stalks Blue Dragon whole lemongrass (from a jar),
      cut into 3 pieces
½   small red onion, peeled and halved
1   dessertspoon dark soft brown sugar
2   pieces jalapeño pepper, from a jar
1   tablespoon Thai fish sauce
1   dessertspoon each sesame oil and groundnut (or similar) oil

FOR THE ORIENTAL DIPPING SAUCE

1   clove garlic, peeled
1   piece jalapeño pepper, from a jar
1   dessertspoon dark soft brown sugar
1   tablespoon lime juice
2   tablespoons each rice vinegar and Thai fish sauce
      green parts of 2 spring onions

Chop all the marinade ingredients in a mini-chopper, then empty them into a bowl. Slice the steak across into thin strips, then add these to the bowl, pushing them down well into the marinade. For the dipping sauce, mini-chop all the ingredients, give them a good burst, then pour the sauce into a bowl.

To cook the steak, heat a frying-pan lightly brushed with oil till very hot, then add the strips of steak. Cook for 30 seconds, then flip them over with a fork and spoon (or tongs) and give them another 30 seconds before transferring to a warm serving dish. To serve: roll up strips of steak, shredded spring onion, cucumber and coriander in the lettuce leaves, swirling them in the dipping sauce – and have plenty of paper napkins handy.

serves 2.

137

quick Thai chicken & coconut curry.

In Thailand, they use cooked chicken in recipes, but if you want to use raw it will cook in the same time.

2	ready-cooked chicken breasts, cut into bite-size pieces
2	tins (each 165ml) Blue Dragon light coconut milk
1	heaped teaspoon cumin seeds
1	dessertspoon coriander seeds
1	medium onion, peeled and cut into chunks
3	cloves garlic, peeled
1	dessertspoon Thai Taste shredded kaffir lime leaves (from a jar)
12	blanched almonds
2	piri piri chillies from a jar (Tesco Ingredients or Waitrose Cooks' Ingredients), stalks removed
1	dessertspoon groundnut or other flavourless oil

FOR THE GARNISH
lime wedges
fresh coriander leaves

Start by crushing the cumin and coriander seeds with a pestle and mortar (or the back of a spoon), then add them to a small hot frying-pan and cook for about 1 minute to release the fragrance. Next, whiz the onion, garlic, lime leaves, almonds, chillies and a little salt in a mini-chopper until very finely chopped.

Now heat the oil in a wide pan over a medium heat, add the spices and chopped ingredients and cook, stirring, for a couple of minutes. Then add the chicken pieces and coconut milk, reduce the heat and cook very gently without a lid for 20 minutes. Serve with Thai jasmine rice, garnished with wedges of lime and coriander leaves.

serves 2.

dhal curry.

This is perfect to serve as a side dish with a meat curry, or for veggies simply to spoon over a mixture of rice and vegetables.

300g   tin green lentils (Tesco), drained and rinsed
1   small red onion, peeled and quartered
1 or 2 cloves garlic, peeled
1   tablespoon groundnut or other flavourless oil
2   teaspoons Seasoned Pioneers Sambhar powder
150ml hot stock made from Marigold bouillon powder
1   rounded tablespoon half-fat crème fraîche

First, chop the onion and garlic together quite finely in a mini-chopper, then heat the oil in a small saucepan, add the chopped ingredients and cook them for 5 minutes. After that, stir in the Sambhar powder and cook for a further 30 seconds before adding the lentils and stock. Season, then simmer gently, uncovered, for 10 minutes. Finally, stir in the crème fraîche and it's ready to serve.

serves 2, or 4 as an accompaniment.

Goan lamb Xacuti.

Our favourite Indian restaurant is the Memsaheb on Thames in the Isle of Dogs, which is where we were first introduced to this wonderful curry.

450g	neck of lamb fillet, trimmed and cut into bite-size pieces
2	tablespoons groundnut or other flavourless oil
50g	desiccated coconut
2	cloves garlic, peeled and crushed
1	large onion, peeled and sliced
5	teaspoons Seasoned Pioneers Goan Xacuti curry powder
275ml	hot stock made from Marigold bouillon powder
1	heaped dessertspoon Seasoned Pioneers tamarind paste

Heat 1 tablespoon of the oil in a frying pan, then add the coconut and garlic and cook over a medium heat (stirring from time to time to prevent it catching) till the coconut has browned – about 5 minutes.

Now, in a medium-size pan, heat the other tablespoon of oil and when it's nice and hot add the onions and stir them around for a minute or so before adding the pieces of meat. Sprinkle in the browned coconut and garlic, followed by the curry powder and some seasoning.

Pour in the stock and give everything a good stir. Finally, stir in the tamarind paste, bring it all up to simmering point and cover with a lid. Cook for 1 hour over a very gentle heat or until the meat is perfectly tender. Serve with basmati rice – and it's great with the coconut sambal on page 122.

serves 2.

winter warmer.

Spanish pork stew with potatoes & chorizo.

lazy braising
duvet days.

for an up-to-date ingredients list go to www.deliaonline.com

Spanish pork stew with potatoes & chorizo.

This and the other recipes in this chapter are weekend stuff.
You assemble the ingredients, whack them into a cooking pot,
then leave them in the oven while you go and do other things:
relax, go back to sleep, read the papers, watch a football match.
This is one of our Sunday lunch favourites.

450g piece trimmed shoulder of pork
450g small salad potatoes, such as Anya (Sainsbury's Taste
the Difference), or similar
110g chorizo sausage (in one piece)
250g Odysea or Karyatis roasted red peppers in oil, drained and halved
1 fat clove garlic, peeled, halved and thinly sliced
1 large red onion, peeled and cut into thick slices
6 sprigs fresh thyme
1 tablespoon olive oil
¼ teaspoon saffron strands
2 tablespoons white wine vinegar (Tesco Finest Chardonnay
white wine vinegar is good)
150ml dry white wine
300g jar Heinz tomato frito
2 heaped tablespoons mixed green and black olives

Pre-heat the oven to gas mark 1, 140°C. What you need to do here is chop the
pork into 2.5cm chunks and pop it straight into a flameproof casserole. Then
chop the chorizo into slightly smaller chunks before you toss it in to join the pork.
Next, add the halved drained peppers, the garlic and the onion. After that, add
the thyme, some seasoning and the olive oil and toss everything together.

Next, using a pestle and mortar (or the back of a spoon), crush the saffron to a
powder and mix with the wine vinegar. Add this to the casserole, followed by the
white wine, tomato frito, olives and the potatoes. Give everything another stir,
put a lid on the casserole and bring up to simmering point on top of the stove,
then transfer the casserole to the oven for 1½ hours. Serve with green beans.

serves 4.

Greek lamb baked with lemon & garlic.

How something so simple can taste so good may be difficult to understand, but it does!

800g   **neck of lamb fillet**
2   **medium lemons**
4   **cloves garlic, peeled**
           large handful fresh flat-leaf parsley

Pre-heat the oven to gas mark 2, 150°C. All you do is trim any excess fat from the lamb and cut it into 2.5cm thick rounds. Now tear off a sheet of foil large enough to wrap them in and place in a roasting tin. Arrange the pieces of meat in the centre of the foil.

Next, slice 3 of the garlic cloves into slivers and, using the tip of a sharp knife, make incisions in the lamb and insert the pieces of garlic, distributing them as evenly as possible. Now grate the zest from the lemons (reserving it for later), squeeze the lemon juice and pour it over the lamb, adding some seasoning.

Fold up the foil to make a parcel, place it in the centre of the oven and cook for 3 hours. Just before serving, chop the remaining clove of garlic and the parsley in a mini-chopper and mix it with the lemon zest. Serve the lamb with the wonderful cooking juices spooned over and sprinkled with the parsley mixture.

note: this is great served with a Greek salad (cucumber chunks, quartered tomatoes, black olives, red onion slices and crumbled feta tossed with olive oil, lemon and garlic), and Oven-sautéed Potatoes with Red Onion, Garlic and Rosemary (page 25).

serves 4.

West African groundnut stew.

After Live Aid in 1986, I helped to produce a book called Food Aid to raise funds. The recipes were contributed by viewers to the Terry Wogan programme and the book was a great hit. This recipe has been adapted from one sent by Kim Yorkshire; I've included it here because it is so good and suits the lazy braiser perfectly.

500g	cubed braising beef
6	tablespoons Whole Earth crunchy organic peanut butter
2	medium onions, peeled and quartered
2	pieces jalapeño pepper, from a jar
1	heaped teaspoon English Provender very lazy ginger
2	heaped teaspooons Seasoned Pioneers African Tsire powder
250g	ready-prepared diced mixed carrot and swede
400g	tin Italian chopped tomatoes
150ml	hot vegetable stock, made with Marigold bouillon powder

Begin by chopping the onions, jalapeño pepper and ginger quite finely in a mini-chopper, then tip them into a bowl and mix with the peanut butter and African Tsire powder, together with some seasoning. Now add the cubes of meat to a medium, flameproof casserole, together with the carrot and swede. Then pour in the tomatoes, peanut butter mixture and stock and give it all a really good stir. Heat up to simmering point, then turn the heat down, cover with a tight-fitting lid and cook very gently, stirring occasionally, for 2 hours or until the meat is tender.

This is nice served with cooked frozen brown rice from Waitrose mixed with a tin of black-eyed beans, heated.

serves 4.

boeuf Bourguignon easy.

Such a cheat this one! In darkest winter, not only is this version better than having no boeuf Bourguignon at all, but it also more than holds its own against the real thing.

500g	cubed braising beef
200g	smoked bacon lardons, or similar
110g	small whole chestnut mushrooms
2	cloves garlic, peeled and sliced
1	medium onion, peeled, halved and sliced
180g	borettane onions in balsamic vinegar (Sainsbury's and Waitrose), drained if necessary
6	sprigs fresh thyme
2	bay leaves
1	heaped tablespoon sauce flour (Sainsbury's or Carrs; see page 248 for stockists), or plain flour
425ml	red Burgundy wine

Pre-heat the oven to gas mark 1, 140°C. This is what you might call an all-in-one recipe – just place the first 8 ingredients in a medium-size, flameproof casserole and season well. Then sprinkle in the flour and, using both hands, toss it all around till everything is lightly coated with flour.

Next, pour in the wine, give it a good stir then – ignoring the most unpromising sight before you – put a close-fitting lid on the casserole. Pop it into the oven on the centre shelf, leave it for 3 hours and look forward to the minimum-effort, maximum-result supper that awaits you. To serve, it needs mounds of fluffy light Aunt Bessie mashed potatoes laced with butter and crème fraîche.

serves 4.

Cincinnati 5-ways chilli.

My friend Matt Gocher, who gave me the original non-cheat recipe, is positively one of the country's leading chilli experts. Here, the chilli is cooked very slowly and, rather than being served with rice, it has five accompaniments: pinto beans (not kidney), grated cheese, raw onion, saltine crackers and soured cream. Here goes.

FOR THE CHILLI
500g cubed braising beef
1 large onion, peeled and quartered
2 cloves garlic, peeled
1 heaped teaspoon each coriander seeds, cumin seeds, ground cinnamon and La Chinata or El Avion smoked hot paprika
350g jar Dress Italian tomato sauce with red pepper and chilli
TO SERVE
400g tin Tarantella organic pinto beans (Co-op)
110g ready-grated mixed Cheddar and mozzarella (Sainsbury's and Tesco)
150ml carton soured cream
 Ritz crackers or saltine crackers
1 large red onion, peeled, quartered and chopped in a mini-chopper

Start off by adding the beef to a medium-size flameproof casserole. Now chop the onion and garlic in a mini-chopper until quite small and add these to the meat. Then crush the coriander and cumin seeds with a pestle and mortar (or the back of a spoon) and add these along with the cinnamon, paprika and seasoning. Finally, pour in the contents of the jar of sauce, then quarter-fill the jar with warm water, put the lid on, give a good shake and add that too. Now bring it all up to simmering point, stirring. Cover with a tight-fitting lid, turn the heat down to its lowest and barely simmer for 4 hours.

To serve, heat the pinto beans in their own juice, drain and rinse them with boiling water and transfer to a warmed bowl. Place the other ingredients in cold dishes, serve the chilli in warm bowls and let everyone help themselves to whatever combination they want. (Matt says you break up the crackers and scatter them in as well.) He likes it hotter, so if you do too, add some chopped piri piri chillies.

serves 4.

curried parsnips.

500g   frozen parsnips
1½   teaspoons Seasoned Pioneers tandoori
     masala spice blend
2   tablespoons groundnut or other
     flavourless oil

Pre-heat the oven to gas mark 6, 200°C. In a mixing
bowl combine the spice blend and some seasoning
with the oil, then toss the frozen parsnips in this mixture to coat them thoroughly. Spread them out on a
baking sheet, then bake for 35-40 minutes.

baked artichoke hearts with lemon vinaigrette.

500g   pack frozen artichoke hearts (Waitrose)
3   tablespoons lemon juice
3   tablespoons olive oil

Pre-heat to gas mark 6, 200°C. In a large bowl, mix
the lemon juice with the olive oil and some seasoning. Then toss the frozen artichoke hearts in this and
spread them out on a baking tray in one layer. Bake
for 35-40 minutes.

warm red bean salad with chorizo.

400g   frozen cooked red kidney beans (Tesco
     Whole Foods)
10cm   chorizo sausage, chopped small
1   small red onion, peeled and quartered
     the equivalent of ½ roasted red pepper
     (from a jar)
1   clove garlic, peeled
3   tablespoons olive oil
1   tablespoon red wine vinegar (Tesco
     Finest Chianti red wine vinegar is good)

Fry the chorizo in a frying-pan until the oil starts to
run. Meanwhile, chop the onion, red pepper and
garlic in a mini-chopper, then add the olive oil and
red wine vinegar and give it one more pulse. Then
add the frozen kidney beans to the chorizo in the pan
and season. Cover and cook over a medium heat for
4-5 minutes or until the beans are soft. Tip into a
bowl and add the dressing while warm.

panic buttons.

Forgot to buy any fresh vegetables for supper? With a few little supplies from your freezer it's soon sorted. Here are a few variations on veg from the freezer which will transform them into something a bit special. (All recipes for 4 people.)

butternut squash with coriander.

500g	pack frozen butternut squash (Waitrose)
2	dessertspoons coriander seeds
2	cloves garlic, crushed
2	tablespoons olive oil

Pre-heat the oven to gas mark 6, 200°C. First crush the coriander seeds with a pestle and mortar or the back of a spoon very finely. Put the seeds in a bowl with the garlic. Arrange the frozen butternut squash chunks in a single layer on a baking tray, then brush each one with olive oil to coat completely. Sprinkle the squash with the garlic and coriander seeds and a little salt, then bake in the oven for 30 minutes.

baby broad beans with bacon.

500g	frozen baby broad beans
1	pack (about 50g) ready-cooked crispy smoked bacon
4	tablespoons olive oil
2	tablespoons white wine vinegar (Tesco Finest Chardonnay white wine vinegar is good)

Steam the frozen beans until tender, then toss them in the olive oil and white wine vinegar. Season them, then crumble in the contents of the pack of crispy bacon and give another good mix before serving.

marinated aubergine with basil.

225g	frozen chargrilled aubergine slices (Asda)
2	tablespoons chopped fresh basil
1½	tablespoons olive oil
1	clove garlic, peeled and crushed
1½	tablespoons Fattorie Giacobazzi Vintage aged balsamic vinegar (Sainsbury's)

Arrange the chargrilled aubergine slices in a single layer in a shallow dish, then cover them with the chopped basil, the oil mixed with the crushed garlic and the balsamic vinegar. Marinate for 45 minutes-1 hour until the aubergine is defrosted (or longer if possible).

veggie?

so now you tell me!

for an up-to-date ingredients list go to www.deliaonline.com

cauliflower cheese & broccoli soup.

A lovely fresh-tasting soup this. You can choose the cheese here — basically whatever you have: Roquefort, Gorgonzola, Cheddar — but this one's made with Parmesan simply because it's always there to hand. Not much cheating, in fact, just a bag of fresh, ready-prepared florets of cauliflower and broccoli, and a tub of fresh ready-grated Parmesan.

1	pack (about 350g) ready-prepared cauliflower and broccoli florets
2	slightly rounded tablespoons fresh ready-grated Parmesan
1	teaspoon butter
1	small onion, peeled, quartered and chopped in a mini-chopper, or 2 tablespoons frozen diced onion
1	bay leaf
	a few gratings whole nutmeg

275ml milk
570ml hot vegetable stock made with Marigold bouillon powder

In a medium saucepan, melt the butter over a low heat, add the onion and soften it for 5 minutes before adding the cauliflower and broccoli. Keeping the heat low, put a lid on and let the vegetables sweat for 10 minutes.

After that, add the rest of the ingredients and some seasoning, stir well, put the lid back on and keep it at the very gentlest simmer for 20 minutes or until the vegetables are tender. Now fish out the bay leaf and purée the soup in the saucepan with a stick blender, tasting to check the seasoning. It's very luscious and creamy, so doesn't need anything to go with it other than some good bread.

serves 2-3, or 4 as a starter.

chickpea soup with whole spices.

This has got quite a zesty, spicy tang to it but if you want a tad more heat, make it 2 pieces of jalapeño pepper instead.

250g	frozen cooked chickpeas (Tesco Whole Foods), defrosted for 10 minutes at room temperature
1	teaspoon cumin seeds
1	teaspoon coriander seeds
1	dessertspoon butter
1	fat clove garlic, peeled and crushed
1	teaspoon ground turmeric
1	piece jalapeño pepper, from a jar, sliced
4-5	sprigs fresh coriander
	grated zest and juice of ½ large lemon
425ml	hot vegetable stock made from Marigold bouillon powder
2	tablespoons half-fat crème fraîche

First, heat a medium saucepan, then add the cumin and coriander seeds. Dry-roast them for 2 minutes and tip them into a mortar. Now heat the butter and the garlic gently together in the warm pan, crush the seeds with the pestle and mortar (or, if you don't have one, the back of a spoon) and return them to the pan, together with the turmeric and sliced jalapeño.

Now add the chickpeas to the pan, followed by the coriander stalks (reserving the leaves), lemon zest, stock and some seasoning. Simmer everything gently with a lid on for 15 minutes then, using a stick blender, whiz the whole lot to a purée and stir in the lemon juice and 1 tablespoon crème fraîche. Serve in warmed bowls with the rest of the crème fraîche swirled in and the coriander leaves sprinkled over to garnish.

serves 2, or 4 as a starter.

patatas Arequipa.

This recipe — one of the best impromptu vegetarian dishes I know — is dedicated to the school in Zapallal, near Lima in Peru, which we have helped to fund for a number of years (see www.zapallal.com).

500g	McCain frozen lightly spiced potato wedges
	about 1 dessertspoon olive oil
6	hardboiled eggs, peeled
half a	285g jar roasted red and yellow peppers (M&S), drained and cut into strips
2	heaped tablespoons pitted black Kalamata olives (Sainsbury's or other)

FOR THE SAUCE

50g	(half a pack) walnut halves
2	piri piri chillies, from a jar (Tesco Ingredients or Waitrose Cooks' Ingredients), stalks removed
1	shallot, peeled and roughly chopped
1	large clove garlic, peeled
2	rounded tablespoons natural cottage cheese
55ml	groundnut or other flavourless oil
75ml	milk
	cayenne pepper
1	dessertspoon white wine vinegar (Tesco Finest Chardonnay white wine vinegar is best)

Pre-heat the oven to gas mark 7, 220°C. Begin by tossing the potato wedges in the olive oil to coat them, then arrange them on a baking tray and roast for 18 minutes. Meanwhile, make the sauce: place the walnuts in a mini-chopper, along with the chillies, shallot, garlic, cottage cheese, oil, milk, a good pinch of cayenne and some salt. Whiz them all together until you have a smooth sauce, transfer to a bowl and stir in the vinegar. Taste to see if more seasoning is needed.

Now arrange the potato wedges in a serving dish, then halve the eggs and place them over the wedges, cut side up. Arrange the pepper strips over the eggs and scatter over the olives, then drizzle some of the sauce over the whole lot. Serve the rest of the sauce in small bowls, sprinkled with a little extra cayenne.

serves 4.

spanakopita.
Greek spinach pasties.

*These have long been one of the delights of our visits to Greece.
Now with the help of our fantastic little rounds of thinly rolled,
light-as-air puff pastry we can revisit them in a flash at any time.*

1	bag (about 225g) young leaf spinach
4	Jus-Rol frozen small individual puff pastry rounds, defrosted for about 15 minutes (covered with a cloth)
1	teaspoon soft butter
2	heaped tablespoons crumbled feta cheese
4	heaped tablespoons fresh ready-grated Parmesan
1	clove garlic, peeled and crushed
1	teaspoon lemon juice
	whole nutmeg, for grating
1	medium egg, beaten, for brushing

Pre-heat the oven to gas mark 7, 220°C. To begin with, microwave the spinach according to the instructions on the pack or cook until just wilted in a large pan; either way, empty it into a colander and leave it to cool. Meanwhile, place the butter, feta, Parmesan, garlic and lemon juice in a bowl. Then, when the spinach is cool enough, squeeze out every last bit of moisture (hands are best for this) and roughly chop it, then combine it with the other ingredients in the bowl, adding some seasoning and a good grating of nutmeg.

Now place a heaped tablespoon of the spinach mixture on to one half of each pastry round, brush the edge with beaten egg, then fold the other half over each one, pressing the edges well together. Transfer the pasties to a greased baking sheet, make a small hole in the centre of each one (to allow the steam to escape), then brush them with more beaten egg. Bake for 15-20 minutes or until golden-brown.

serves 2.

pasta supper.

seafood linguine.

pronto italiano
bye-bye-pizza takeaways.

for an up-to-date ingredients list go to www.deliaonline.com

pasta faster.

Pasta in our kitchen has changed beyond recognition. No more slaving over sauces, no more long simmering sessions. Now that we can buy outstanding Italian tomato-based sauces, slowly reduced using fresh Italian tomatoes, on busy days we can arrive home and have an authentic pasta dish made in minutes. Below and on the next page are our top three favourites.

seafood linguine.

If ever you wanted proof of how food from the freezer can save you so much time – and produce a stunning result – look no further than this truly great pasta dish.

225g	mixed frozen raw seafood selection or fruits de mer from a pack (such as prawns, squid and mussels)
120g	jar baby clams, drained (L'Isola d'Oro are good; see page 248 for stockists)
225g	dried linguine (Col Sapori di Napoli is my favourite; see page 248 for stockists)
1	tablespoon olive oil
2	large cloves garlic, peeled and crushed
1	dessertspoon chopped fresh rosemary
2	tablespoons dry vermouth
350g	jar Dress Italian tomato sauce with sun-dried tomato

First, cook the linguine in 2.25 litres boiling salted water for 8-10 minutes (check on the pack) until *al dente*. Meanwhile, heat the oil in a medium saucepan, add the garlic and rosemary, stir them around and cook over a medium heat for a couple of minutes before adding the vermouth and continuing to cook for another minute. After that, stir in the mixed frozen seafood and the drained clams and toss them around the pan for 2-3 more minutes, or until the prawns have turned pink and opaque on both sides. Finally, pour in the sun-dried tomato sauce, season and stir to mix everything well. Simmer gently for 5 minutes.

Drain the linguine in a colander and divide between 2 warmed serving dishes. Serve with the seafood sauce.

serves 2.

puttanesca presto.

There are two ways to go here: you can whiz the ingredients in a mini-chopper in no time at all, or Waitrose does a jar of ready-made puttanesca mix, which can be used to replace the olives, capers and anchovies.

400g	dried Martelli maccheroni or Col Sapori di Napoli penne a triangolo (see page 248 for stockists)
150g	pitted black Kalamata olives (Sainsbury's or other)
1	heaped tablespoon capers, rinsed and drained
50g	tinned anchovy fillets in extra virgin olive oil (Sainsbury's)
2	piri piri chillies, from a jar (Tesco Ingredients or Waitrose Cooks' Ingredients), stalks removed and chopped
350g	jar Dress Italian tomato sauce with sun-dried tomato
2	tablespoons red wine
	handful of fresh basil leaves, chopped
	fresh ready-grated Parmesan

Cook the pasta in 2.25 litres boiling, salted water for 10 minutes. Meanwhile, warm 2 pasta bowls and make the puttanesca sauce. Place the olives, capers, anchovies (with their oil) and the piri piri chillies in a mini-chopper and pulse-chop roughly.

Then transfer this puttanesca mix to a medium saucepan. Add the tomato sauce, then rinse out the jar with the wine and add that, together with the basil and some seasoning. Then just leave the sauce to simmer gently until the pasta is ready. Drain the pasta in a colander, then quickly return it to the pan and mix in the sauce. Serve in warm bowls, with lots of Parmesan to sprinkle over.

serves 4.

the best spaghetti Bolognese.

While certainly the very best cheats' version, this is also one of the fastest and nicest storecupboard recipes in the book.

225g	Martelli spaghetti (see page 248 for stockists), or other top-quality dried pasta
220g	tin minced beef (M&S)
350g	jar Dress Italian tomato sauce with basil and onion
2	tablespoons red wine
	handful of fresh basil leaves, chopped
	fresh ready-grated Parmesan

Cook the spaghetti in 2.25 litres boiling, salted water for 10 minutes. Meanwhile, warm 2 pasta bowls and make the sauce by emptying the contents of the jar of sauce into a pan, along with the minced beef. Rinse out the jar with the wine and add that to the pan, together with some seasoning. Then, just leave the sauce to simmer gently until the pasta is ready. Drain the spaghetti in a colander, divide between the bowls, spoon over the sauce and sprinkle with the fresh basil and lots of Parmesan.

serves 2.

spinach tortelloni with leeks & Gorgonzola.

The tortelloni used here can be frozen, so it's a good idea to have some spares tucked away as this is really something quite special for two, when time is short.

300g	pack fresh spinach and ricotta tortelloni (Tesco or Sainsbury's)
2	medium leeks, cleaned, cut in half lengthways and chopped small
200g	Gorgonzola Piccante, cut into cubes
200ml	tub half-fat crème fraîche
	whole nutmeg, for grating
1	heaped tablespoon dried breadcrumbs (Waitrose Cooks' Ingredients) or dried ciabatta breadcrumbs (Tesco Ingredients)
1	heaped tablespoon fresh ready-grated Parmesan

First, in a wide pan, heat the crème fraîche, then add the leeks along with some seasoning. Keep the heat low and let them cook gently for about 7-8 minutes without a lid or until tender.

Meanwhile pre-heat the grill and fill a saucepan with 1.5 litres boiling water, add some salt and bring it up to the boil. Now give the leeks a stir, grate in about ⅓ of the whole nutmeg and remove them from the heat.

When the water bubbles, add the tortelloni and time it to cook for 2 minutes. After that, drain it quickly in a colander then, leaving some of the water clinging to it, tip it into the saucepan to join the leeks. Give it all a good stir, then, using a spatula, spoon it into a gratin dish, stirring in half the Gorgonzola and scattering the rest on top.

Finally, mix the breadcrumbs and grated Parmesan together, then sprinkle this all over, whack it under the grill about 10cm from the heat and give it 3-5 minutes, or until the sauce is bubbling and the crumbs are brown and crisp. Serve in warm bowls. A leafy salad with raw strips of fennel and a lemony dressing would be good with this.

serves 2.

such a tart!

tricks & treats.

for an up-to-date ingredients list go to www.deliaonline.com

thick onion tart with cheese & sage.

I can still hardly believe how very simple this is, and indeed the other versions that follow. After years of making, resting and rolling pastry, lining tins and pre-baking, life has moved on and now I can make these lovely recipes even on busy days. Although the pastry cases are bought fresh, I keep a stock of them in the freezer and always fill and cook them straight from frozen, adding 5 minutes to the cooking time.

230g	Jus-Rol fresh large shortcrust pastry case
390g	tin Eazy fried onions
1	tablespoon fresh ready-grated mature Cheddar
3	dessertspoons fresh ready-grated Parmesan
1	dessertspoon chopped fresh sage, plus 8 fresh sage leaves
150ml	double or single cream
2	eggs

Pre-heat the oven to gas mark 6, 200°C. First, pop a baking sheet into the centre of the oven while it's pre-heating. Then empty the onions into a sieve set over a bowl and press them with the back of a tablespoon to extract as much juice as possible. Now whisk the cream and eggs together in a jug, add the Cheddar, 2 dessertspoons of the Parmesan, the chopped sage and some seasoning, then give everything a really good mix.

Using an oven glove, remove the baking sheet from the oven, place the pastry case, still in its foil container, on it and scatter the onions over the base. Then pour the filling in, arrange 8 sage leaves in a circle on top and, finally, scatter the rest of the Parmesan over. Carefully return the baking tray to the centre of the oven, reduce the heat to gas mark 4, 180°C and cook the tart for 35-40 minutes or until golden and puffy and the centre feels firm. Leave to settle for 10 minutes before serving cut into wedges, with dressed watercress.

note: this can also be made in 6 Jus-Rol frozen tartlet cases; cook as above.

serves 4-6.

Roquefort & leek tart.

Another variation on the theme of almost-instant tarts, this one combining a lovely creaminess with a certain piquancy from the Roquefort. (Perfect for veggies too.)

230g	Jus-Rol fresh large shortcrust pastry case
100g	Roquefort, Shropshire Blue or Cashel Blue
225g	leeks (about 2 medium leeks), trimmed, washed and thinly sliced
1	tablespoon butter
4	spring onions, including the green parts, chopped
225ml	double cream
2	eggs
1	tablespoon fresh ready-grated Parmesan

Pre-heat the oven to gas mark 6, 200°C. First, pop a baking sheet into the centre of the oven while it's pre-heating. Meanwhile, melt the butter in a frying-pan, add the chopped spring onions and leeks and cook them over a medium heat for 5-6 minutes. Now, using oven gloves, place the pastry case, still in its foil container, on the baking sheet, arrange the onion-and-leek mixture over the base and crumble the Roquefort on top.

Whisk the double cream and the eggs together in a jug, season and then pour this over the cheese and leeks. Sprinkle the Parmesan over the surface, then transfer the baking sheet to the centre of the oven. Reduce the heat to gas mark 4, 180°C and bake the tart for 35-40 minutes, till golden and firm in the centre. Leave to rest for 10 minutes before serving with a tossed green salad.

note: this can also be made in 6 Jus-Rol frozen tartlet cases; cook as above.

serves 4-6.

Cromer crab tart.

If you can't lay your hands on a dressed Cromer crab, the tinned alternative is more than acceptable. This recipe also works well using 250g smoked salmon trimmings instead of the crab but omit the sherry and the Parmesan and add a little freshly grated nutmeg to the mixture.

230g   Jus-Rol fresh large shortcrust pastry case
1   medium fresh dressed Cromer crab, or 2 x 170g tins jumbo
       crab meat (Asda Extra Special) or other white crab meat
2   eggs, beaten
1   tablespoon dry sherry
       cayenne pepper
200ml tub half-fat crème fraîche
2   rounded tablespoons fresh ready-grated Parmesan

Pre-heat the oven to gas mark 6, 200°C. First, pop a baking sheet into the centre of the oven while it's pre-heating. Remove the crab meat from the shell (or drain, if using tins) and tip into a mixing bowl. Now combine the crab meat with the eggs, sherry, ¼ teaspoon cayenne, the crème fraîche and 1½ rounded tablespoons of the Parmesan. Add some seasoning and mix thoroughly.

Using oven gloves, place the pastry case, still in its foil container, on the pre-heated baking sheet, then pour the crab mixture into the pastry case and sprinkle with the remaining Parmesan and a pinch of cayenne. Return to the centre of the oven and reduce the heat to gas mark 4, 180°C, then bake for 35-40 minutes or until golden, puffy and just set in the centre. Allow the tart to settle for about 10 minutes before serving. I think this is lovely served with a green salad with lots of watercress.

note: this can also be made in 6 Jus-Rol frozen tartlet cases; cook as above.

serves 4-6.

magic tarts.

These are so named because they are such a breeze: no making pastry, no rolling out, no lining tins — nothing but the thinnest ready-rolled rounds of melt-in-the-mouth pastry, sitting quietly in the freezer waiting to be summoned for a quick starter or a light lunch. I've included a variety of filling ideas here, but once you get hooked, no doubt you'll find all kinds of permutations for yourself.

Portabello mushroom, chorizo & thyme tarts.

2   Jus-Rol frozen small individual puff pastry rounds, defrosted
         for about 15 minutes (covered with a cloth)
2   Portabello mushrooms
         a few small sprigs of fresh thyme
50g   chorizo sausage, sliced
         olive oil
         1 medium egg, beaten

Pre-heat the oven to gas mark 6, 200°C. Begin this one by oiling a small baking tray, then place the mushrooms on it, sprinkle each one with a few drops of olive oil, and season. Then pop them in the oven and pre-cook for 10 minutes. After that, remove them and allow to cool for about 20 minutes.

To cook the tarts, brush each pastry round with some of the beaten egg, place a cooled mushroom in the centre and arrange slices of chorizo on top in an over-lapping circle. Bring the pastry edges up all round and pinch the edges to form a border. Now use a palette knife to transfer the tarts to the baking tray, brush the edges all round with beaten egg and place a few sprigs of thyme on top. Bake for 15-20 minutes till golden-brown and puffy. Serve hot with dressed salad leaves.

serves 2.

209

Parma ham, fig & Gorgonzola tarts.

2	Jus-Rol frozen small individual puff pastry rounds, defrosted for 15 minutes (covered with a cloth)
6	slices Parma ham (Sainsbury's Taste the Difference 24-month matured Parma ham is good)
4	figs, quartered
50g	Gorgonzola
	oil for greasing
1	medium egg, beaten

Pre-heat the oven to gas mark 6, 200°C. Begin by greasing a small, solid baking tray quite generously. Now arrange the pastry rounds on the tray, brush each one with some of the beaten egg and arrange the Parma ham all over, taking it right up to the edges and folding it here and there to make it fit. Next, arrange 8 sections of fig in the centre of each one, divide the cheese in half and scatter small pieces over the figs.

Now bring the edges of the pastry up to make a kind of border, folding them over at the top and pinching the folds together – it's all quite haphazard, so don't worry if it doesn't look perfectly neat. Add some freshly milled pepper at this point, then finally brush the pastry all round the edge with beaten egg.

Pop them on to a high shelf in the oven and bake till puffy and golden-brown, about 15-20 minutes. Serve warm with dressed salad leaves.

serves 2.

Piedmont pepper tarts.

2	Jus-Rol frozen small individual puff pastry rounds, defrosted for 15 minutes (covered with a cloth)
2	large strips from a jar of Odysea or Karyatis roasted red peppers, drained and halved
2	medium firm, ripe tomatoes
1	medium egg, beaten
6	anchovy fillets in extra virgin olive oil (Sainsbury's), drained
1	tablespoon chopped fresh basil leaves, plus 2 fresh basil sprigs, to garnish
2	cloves garlic, peeled and thinly sliced

Pre-heat the oven to gas mark 6, 200°C. First, place the tomatoes in a bowl, pour boiling water over them and after 1 minute drain off the water, slip the skins off and cut each tomato in half.

Now arrange the pastry rounds on a small, solid, greased baking tray and brush each one with some of the beaten egg, then pat any excess oil from the peppers with kitchen paper. Lay the peppers on the pastry rounds, followed by 2 halves of tomato on each and then 3 anchovy fillets (each one snipped into pieces with scissors). Next, scatter the basil leaves and garlic slices on top, add some seasoning and a little drizzle of oil (from the jar of peppers). Bring the pastry up all round, pinching the folds to form a border, and brush the pastry generously with beaten egg.

Now, bake on a high shelf in the oven for 15-20 minutes until golden-brown and puffy. Garnish each tart with a basil sprig and serve hot, straight from the oven, with dressed salad leaves.

serves 2.

classic quiche Lorraine.

Never has a quiche Lorraine — essentially an egg, bacon and cream tart — been so easy to make, without losing any of its classic flavour and texture.

230g   Jus-Rol fresh large shortcrust pastry case
2   eggs
1   pack (about 50g) ready-cooked crispy smoked bacon
225ml double cream
3   tablespoons ready-grated mature Cheddar
1   tablespoon fresh ready-grated Parmesan

Pre-heat the oven to gas mark 6, 200°C. First, pop a baking sheet into the centre of the oven while it's pre-heating. Meanwhile, beat the eggs with the cream in a jug and season. Next, crumble the crispy bacon over the base of the pastry case and sprinkle over the Cheddar.

Using oven gloves, remove the baking sheet from the oven and place the pastry case, still in its foil container, on it. Pour in the egg-and-cream mixture and sprinkle the grated Parmesan over the surface. Now return the baking sheet to the centre of the oven, reduce the heat to gas mark 4, 180°C and bake the quiche for 35-40 minutes till golden and firm in the centre. Leave to rest for 10 minutes before serving, perhaps with a classic tomato salad.

note: this can also be made in 6 Jus-Rol frozen tartlet cases; cook as above.

serves 4-6.

chocolate tartlets.

We've sometimes made this in one large M&S tart case – the choice is yours. Either way, these are very pretty, with a wonderfully glossy surface, but you could give them a dusting of cocoa.

192g   pack of 8 all-butter sweet tartlet cases (M&S)
320g   jar Fairtrade rich chocolate truffle sauce (M&S)
50g   unsalted butter
2   tablespoons half-fat crème fraîche
1   tablespoon Cognac (or dark rum)
     well-chilled pouring cream or crème fraîche, to serve

Start off by putting the chocolate truffle sauce, butter, crème fraîche and Cognac into a heatproof bowl, then place the bowl over a pan of barely simmering water, making sure the base of the bowl doesn't actually touch the water. Heat gently, until smooth and glossy, stirring now and then.

Now pour the chocolate mixture into the tartlet cases. Leave them to cool before covering and chilling in the fridge for a minimum of 1½ hours. Serve with a generous amount of cream or crème fraîche.

serves 8.

Portuguese custard tarts.

These are perfect to serve warm as a dessert, although I personally prefer them chilled. Either way, they just melt in the mouth, with pastry as light as a whisper and a filling of wobbly custard flavoured with vanilla, caramel and cinnamon.

4	Jus-Rol frozen small individual puff pastry rounds, defrosted for 15 minutes (covered with a cloth)
1	tablespoon custard powder
1	tablespoon golden caster sugar
	100ml milk
3	egg yolks, plus 1 medium egg, beaten, for brushing
	200ml half-fat crème fraîche
1½	teaspoons vanilla extract (Ndali Fairtrade vanilla extract is best; see page 248 for stockists)
½	teaspoon ground cinnamon
1	tablespoon Vahiné caramel sauce, from a 210g bottle (see page 248 for stockists)

Pre-heat the oven to gas mark 6, 200°C. First make the custard, which is so easy: place the custard powder and sugar in a bowl and mix it to a smooth paste with the milk and egg yolks. Then heat the crème fraîche in a saucepan and, when it begins to bubble, pour it in to join the custard powder mixture. Whisk everything together, then return it to the saucepan and, still whisking, bring it up to a simmer. When it begins to boil it will become thick, so remove it from the heat, add the vanilla extract, then pour it into a bowl and allow to cool.

When the custard is cold, brush the pastry rounds with some of the beaten egg and transfer them (using a palette knife) to a well-greased baking sheet. Now spoon some of the cold custard into the centre of each one, leaving a 2.5cm border all round. Bring up the edges of the pastry to form into tarts, pinching and sealing the folds.

Brush the pastry with more beaten egg, sprinkle with cinnamon and bake for 15-20 minutes till the pastry is dark golden-brown. The filling will puff up quite a lot, but it will soon sink back as it cools. Finally, brush each one with caramel sauce to give a shiny glaze over the filling and pastry. These are best eaten as fresh as possible.

serves 4.

tea party.

chocolate cake

sweet cheats
ending on a high.

chocolate cupcakes.

Absolutely no fear whatsoever attached to making these fab but easy home-made cakes. No creaming or curdling and the mashed potato makes them wonderfully moist. We've also tested this as one large cake (see below), so if you need a new celebration cake, this is it.

150g	Green & Black's organic dark chocolate (85% cocoa solids)
110g	condensed milk from a 397g tin
110g	light muscovado sugar
150g	unsalted butter
6	discs Aunt Bessie's Homestyle frozen mashed potato, defrosted
200g	self-raising flour, sifted
2	teaspoons baking powder
1-2	teaspoons Chinese five-spice powder
2	eggs

FOR THE CHOCOLATE ICING

150g	Green & Black's organic dark chocolate (85% cocoa solids)
	the rest of the condensed milk from the 397g tin
50g	soft unsalted butter
48	pink chocolate buttons (see page 248 for stockists)

Pre-heat the oven to gas mark 4, 180°C. Fill two 12-hole patty tins with 24 cupcake cases. To make the cakes, place the chocolate, broken up, in a large, heatproof bowl along with the condensed milk, sugar and butter, then set this over a saucepan of simmering water, making sure the base of the bowl doesn't touch the water. Then, keeping the heat at its lowest, allow the ingredients to melt slowly, stirring occasionally. It should take about 5 minutes to become smooth, then remove it from the heat and leave to cool for 5 minutes.

Now put the remaining cake ingredients in a large bowl, add the chocolate mixture and mix everything with an electric whisk till smooth. Divide among the cupcake cases, then bake on the centre shelf for about 15 minutes. Leave in the tins to cool. For the icing, break the chocolate into a heatproof bowl, add the condensed milk and melt them together, as above. Then take the bowl off the heat and stir in the butter until melted. Leave the mixture to cool for 5 minutes, then use it to top the cakes. Finish each one with 2 pink chocolate buttons.

makes 24. note: to make 1 large cake, use 2 x 20cm lightly greased and lined tins and cook for 30 minutes. When cool, make the icing and use a third of it to sandwich the cakes and the rest over the top and around the sides.

225

chocolate ricotta mousse.

Not technically a mousse as such, I confess, but every bit as good without the fiddle or fuss.

150g   **dark chocolate (70-75% cocoa solids)**
250g   **tub ricotta cheese**
1   **tablespoon rum**
2   **tablespoons soft dark brown sugar**
200ml **tub half-fat crème fraîche**

Break 100g of the chocolate into a heatproof bowl and place over a pan of simmering water, making sure the base of the bowl doesn't touch the water. Leave for a few minutes, stirring occasionally until the chocolate has melted.

Now place the remaining chocolate, broken into pieces, into a mini-chopper. Chop the chocolate, then remove it and keep to one side. Next, put the ricotta cheese, rum, sugar and 2 tablespoons of the crème fraîche into the bowl of the mini-chopper and blend until completely smooth. Add this to the melted chocolate and mix until the chocolate is incorporated.

Finally, stir in all but 1 tablespoon of the chopped chocolate and divide the mousse among 4 glasses or cups. Top with the remaining crème fraîche and chopped chocolate, cover loosely with clingfilm and chill until ready to serve.

serves 4.

coffee ricotta mousse.

A variation on the Chocolate Ricotta Mousse recipe (left), here given quite a dark, adult coffee flavour.

50g	**Lindt Excellence Coffee Intense chocolate, or similar**
2	**tablespoons instant coffee**
250g	**tub ricotta cheese**
2	**tablespoons soft light brown sugar**
200ml	**tub half-fat crème fraîche**

Place the chocolate, broken into pieces, in a mini-chopper. Chop the chocolate, then remove and keep to one side. Now blend the coffee, 2 tablespoons boiling water and the sugar in a bowl. Reserve 4 teaspoons of the crème fraîche, then add the ricotta cheese and the rest of the crème fraîche to the coffee mixture in the bowl and mix until smooth.

Lastly, stir in all but 1 tablespoon of the chopped chocolate and divide among 4 small glasses or cups. Top with the reserved crème fraîche, sprinkle with the rest of the chopped chocolate, cover loosely with clingfilm and chill in the fridge until ready to serve.

serves 4.

Kaiserschmarrn.
caramelised pancakes with sour cherries.

These were Austrian emperor Franz Joseph's favourite pancakes – and delightful they are too. He ate them with sultanas, but I think dried cherries are even better. And his chefs wouldn't have had the benefit of buying ready-made pancakes, so it's not half the bother it was then.

6	ready-made thin pancakes (not more than 20cm in diameter)
2	tablespoons dark rum
110g	dried cherries
50g	unsalted butter
110g	ready-toasted flaked almonds
2	tablespoons unrefined icing sugar
1	teaspoon ground cinnamon

Begin by warming the rum in a small pan, then add the dried cherries. Remove the pan from the heat and leave on one side for about 15 minutes for the cherries to soften and plump up. Meanwhile, stack the pancakes and, using a sharp knife, cut them all together into strips lengthways and then across so you end up with small squares. Next, pre-heat the grill to its highest setting.

Now melt the butter in a large frying-pan and, when it starts to foam, add the pieces of pancake and the cherry-and-rum mixture, followed by the almonds. Cook over a medium heat for 3-4 minutes, tossing and turning the mixture till it's hot and golden.

Then, sift the icing sugar and cinnamon over the top. Place under the grill for a few minutes until the sugar starts to caramelise and serve immediately with chilled pouring cream, crème fraîche or vanilla ice cream.

serves 4.

no-cook cheesecakes with caramelised rhubarb.

Without doubt this is one of the easiest ways to produce some brilliant cheesecakes without any of the whisking or cooking and so on. You will have to partly freeze them to firm them up, but even that's better than all the fiddle.

450g	curd cheese (Waitrose, Sainsbury's or from deli counters)
4	good-quality stem ginger cookies
1	heaped tablespoon golden caster sugar
1	teaspoon vanilla extract (Ndali Fairtrade vanilla extract is best; see page 248 for stockists)

FOR THE CARAMELISED RHUBARB

450g	ready-prepared fresh rhubarb, cut into small chunks
2	rounded tablespoons unrefined demerara sugar

The most essential ingredient here comes in the shape of 4 ramekins, each with a diameter of 7.5cm. All you do is pop a cookie into each one and, if it seems fractionally too big, trim it round the edges and place the spare crumbs on top. Now combine the curd cheese, sugar and vanilla in a bowl, then spoon the mixture into the ramekins, cover each one with clingfilm and freeze for 45 minutes.

Meanwhile, pre-heat the grill to its highest setting for 10 minutes, line a grill pan with foil, scatter the chunks of rhubarb over it and sprinkle with the sugar. Grill the rhubarb about 10cm from the heat source for 10-15 minutes, turning once, until cooked through and caramelised.

To serve, slide a small palette knife all round the edge of each ramekin, turn out on to serving plates, invert, then spoon the rhubarb on top. The cheesecakes will still be slightly frozen but that's how they should be. You can make these up to 8 hours ahead. If you do this, leave them in the fridge then freeze them for 45 minutes before serving.

serves 4.

cheats' Eton mess.

The meringues from M&S and Asda are made with nothing more than sugar and egg white – which is precisely how you would make them at home. They are a must-have for cheats in the summer soft-fruit season: we love this recipe with raspberries too.

96g   pack of 12 meringue nests (M&S and Asda Extra Special)
450g   strawberries
1   rounded tablespoon unrefined icing sugar
500g   tub Greek yoghurt

First, hull and halve all the strawberries, then place half of them in a mini-chopper with the icing sugar. Whiz to a purée and then pour this into a nylon sieve set over a bowl, pressing the purée through the sieve to remove the seeds. All this can be done in advance.

To serve, what you do is break the meringues up into small pieces into a large mixing bowl. Then add the halved strawberries and fold in the yoghurt. Next, carefully fold in all but about 2 tablespoons of the purée to give a sort of marbled effect. Finally, pile the whole lot into glasses or serving dishes, spoon the rest of the purée over the surface and serve straightaway.

serves 6.

cheats' crème caramel.

OK then, no more sticky moments and saucepans coated in hard toffee. You can, and will, achieve a light, creamy caramel with the utmost of ease — because someone else has made the caramel for you.

210g	bottle Vahiné caramel sauce (see page 248 for stockists)
150ml	milk
275ml	single cream
4	eggs
40g	soft brown sugar
½	teaspoon vanilla extract (Ndali Fairtrade vanilla extract is best - see page 248 for stockists)

Pre-heat the oven to gas mark 2, 150°C. First, pour the caramel sauce into an 850ml ovenproof dish to cover the base. Then, combine the milk and cream in a saucepan and heat them gently. Meanwhile, in a bowl, whisk together the eggs, sugar and vanilla extract, then pour the hot milk and cream in to join them and give another good whisk.

Pour all of this into the dish, place it in a small roasting tin, then pour enough boiling water into the tin to come about two-thirds of the way up. Transfer it to the oven and cook on the centre shelf for 1 hour.

When the crème caramel has cooled, chill it well in the fridge. To serve, you will need a serving dish deep enough to cope with the caramel sauce. Slide a palette knife all round the edge before inverting it on to the serving dish. Serve, cut into wedges with lots of sauce poured over – some chilled pouring cream would make it even more special.

serves 4-6.

Morello cherry & almond crumble.

This is my best crumble and one of the nicest fruits to use is Asda frozen Morello cherries. But any fresh fruit can be used, from apples, apricots (pictured), plums or fresh raspberries.

40g	well-chilled butter
75g	self-raising flour
50g	whole unblanched almonds
50g	unrefined demerara sugar
1	teaspoon ground cinnamon
450g	frozen Morello cherries (Asda) or other fruit
1½	tablespoons unrefined demerara sugar

Pre-heat the oven to gas mark 6, 200°C. For the crumble, all you do is place the butter, cut into chunks, in a mini-chopper, then add the flour and whiz the two together to the fine-crumb stage. Empty this mixture into a bowl. After that, add the nuts to the mini-chopper and pulse-chop until they are roughly chopped (it's important not to chop them too small), then add these to the bowl as well. Stir in the sugar and cinnamon and that's it.

Place your chosen fruit, frozen or fresh, in a round dish 16cm in diameter, or similar, and sprinkle over or stir in the demerara sugar. Sprinkle the crumble mixture on top and press down quite firmly, then bake on the centre shelf of the oven for 40-45 minutes or till well-browned and crisp on top.

Serve with cream, crème fraîche or ready-made vanilla custard.

serves 2-3.

fast fruit brûlée.

Now that fruits are blast-frozen and can be stashed away in the freezer, you can make a sublime fast fruit brûlée or pop them under the grill sprinkled with liqueur and sugar and summon up a caramelised fruit dessert any old time. Both recipes serve 4.

450g pack British garden fruits (Waitrose) or similar, fresh or frozen
about 2 tablespoons golden caster sugar (depending on the fruit you're using)
500g tub Greek yoghurt
75g   unrefined demerara sugar

Place the fruit in a saucepan with the caster sugar, then cook over a gentle heat until the juices run (about 3-5 minutes for fresh fruit and up to 15 minutes for frozen – use a small skewer to test if the fruit is tender). Then drain off the excess juice and reserve it. Tip the fruit into a baking dish, about 18cm square, and stir in 2 tablespoons of the reserved juice, then leave it to cool. Pre-heat the grill for 10 minutes at its highest setting. Spread the yoghurt over to cover the fruit completely, sprinkle the demerara sugar all over and place under the grill (7.5cm from the heat) for 4-5 minutes or until the sugar has melted and it is brown and bubbling. Let it stand for 10 minutes before serving.

or anytime grilled caramelised fruits.

450g of one of the following frozen fruit:
Summer fruit berries, Black Forest fruits, Tropical fruit smoothie mix, Bramley apple and blackberry, or ready-prepared rhubarb
2   tablespoons rum or brandy (or any other liqueur)
about 2 tablespoons golden caster sugar (depending on the fruit you're using)

Pre-heat the grill to its highest setting for 10 minutes. Place the frozen fruit in a shallow, heatproof dish, about 18cm square, drizzle over the rum, then sprinkle with sugar. Grill for about 10-15 minutes or until the sugar has melted and caramelised and the fruit is tender. Serve with ice-cream or crème fraîche.

rich fruit bread & butter pudding.

M&S does a very good rich fruit loaf that is, conveniently, ready sliced. Don't forget to put lots of freshly grated nutmeg on the top and this is extra special if you serve it with chilled Jersey cream.

400g	sliced rich fruit loaf (M&S)
50g	soft butter
4	eggs
350ml	milk
75ml	double cream
60g	golden caster sugar
	grated zest 1 lemon
	whole nutmeg, for grating

Pre-heat the oven to gas 4, 180°C. All you do here is butter the fruit loaf slices, including the crusts, quite liberally and cut each slice in half. Now arrange the slices, overlapping one another, in a well-buttered 18cm x 25.5cm baking dish. Then whisk the eggs in a mixing bowl and add the milk, cream, sugar and lemon zest and give another good whisk. Pour this all over the fruit loaf slices. Grate half the whole nutmeg generously all over, bake in the oven for 35-40 minutes and serve it straight from the oven.

serves 6.

rhubarb & ginger beer jellies.

Packet jellies get the grown-up treatment for these two recipes. This one is lovely in summer, while the lime coconut jellies make a great end to a spicy Asian meal.

450g	fresh rhubarb
2	bottles (each 275ml) Fentimans traditional ginger beer
50g	golden caster sugar
1	heaped teaspoon freshly grated ginger
135g	pack Hartley's orange jelly
200ml	tub half-fat crème fraîche
3	pieces preserved stem ginger

First of all, chop the rhubarb and wash it in cold water, then put it in a medium saucepan with the sugar and freshly grated ginger and heat gently over a lowish heat, which will allow the rhubarb to poach in its own juice until it's soft – 10-15 minutes (it probably won't stay in whole pieces and may look rather smashed, but that doesn't matter).

While that's all happening, break the orange jelly into cubes and put them into a microwaveable measuring jug. Add 3 tablespoons water and heat in the microwave on full power for 1-1 ½ minutes. When the jelly has dissolved, make the liquid quantity in the jug up to 510ml with the ginger beer (you will have some ginger beer left over, cook's perk...).

Next, combine the liquid mixture with the cooked rhubarb, stir everything together and pour the mixture into 6 glasses, each 200ml. (I like to use Manhattan-style glasses but any glass will do.)

Allow the jellies to cool, then cover the top of each glass with clingfilm and transfer them to the fridge to set for about 4-6 hours (or you can leave them overnight if you prefer). To serve the jellies, top each one with a dessertspoon of crème fraîche and a little stem ginger chopped quite small.

serves 6.

lime coconut jellies with mango.

400ml tin light coconut milk
135g   pack Hartley's lime jelly
      finely grated zest and juice 1 lime
FOR THE MANGO SAUCE
425g   tin sliced mangoes in syrup (M&S)
      grated zest and juice of 1 lime
1   heaped teaspoon unrefined icing sugar

First of all, place the jelly cubes in a bowl, add the lime zest and juice and 150ml boiling water. Whisk vigorously to dissolve the jelly. Then add the tin of coconut milk to the mixture, whisk again and divide the mixture equally among 4 polythene mini puddings basins, each 150ml (see page 248 for stockists), or ramekins. Cover each one with clingfilm and chill in the fridge for 4-6 hours, or overnight is fine.

Meanwhile, to make the sauce, place the drained mango in a mini-chopper and whiz to a purée with the lime zest, juice and icing sugar.

To serve the jellies, dip the basins or ramekins very briefly into a small bowl of hot water, then turn the jellies out on to serving plates and drizzle a little mango sauce over and around each one.

serves 4.

top cheats.

These ingredients are my personal favourites.

storecupboard.

Asda Extra Special bonfire rub, Extra Special
  jumbo crab meat
Baxters lobster bisque
Belazu preserved lemons
Blue Dragon light coconut milk, whole
  lemongrass, Vietnamese spring roll wrappers
Buttermilk pancakes
Carrs sauce flour, Sainsbury's sauce flour
Chargrilled artichoke hearts
Coco López cream of coconut
Col Sapori di Napoli dried linguine/penne
Delicias chilli peppers
Dress Italian tomato sauces: with basil and onion, red
  pepper and chilli and sun-dried tomato; red
  pepper and walnut pesto
Eazy fried onions
El Avion sweet or hot smoked paprika
English Provender Company very lazy caramelised
  red onions, very lazy ginger
Epicure organic lentils, black beans
Fattorie Giacobazzi vintage aged balsamic vinegar
Fruttibosco antipasto/dried porcini
Hartley's orange and lime-flavour jellies
Heinz tomato frito
John West dressed crabmeat/dressed lobster meat
Karyatis mixed hot chillies /roasted red peppers
L' Isola d'Oro baby clams
La Chinata sweet or hot smoked paprika
M&S croutons or bruschettine, Chablis white wine
  sauce, chunky chicken in white sauce, Fairtrade
  chocolate truffle sauce, individual all butter
  savoury & sweet pastry tartlet cases, large sweet
  pastry case, meringue nests, minced beef/lamb,
  pear quarters in grape juice, rich caramel toffee
  sauce, rich fruit loaf , roasted red & yellow
  peppers in oil, sliced mangoes in syrup,
  steak & kidney
Martelli dried maccheroni/spaghetti/penne

Ndali Fairtrade vanilla extract
Odysea stuffed vine leaves, aubergine meze,
  gigantes beans in tomato sauce, roasted
  red peppers
Ortiz Spanish tuna
Patak's coconut cream
Perard du Touquet soupe de poissons
Ready-cooked polenta
Sainsbury's anchovy fillets, borettane onions, chair
  de tomate, pitted black Kalamata olives
Seasoned Pioneers spices: Goan Xacuti, Caribbean
  Poudre de Colombo, Ras-el-Hanout, Sambhar
  powder, tandoori masala, African Tsire,
  Indonesian 'Seven Seas', cardamom masala,
  tamarind paste, Thai shrimp paste
Soreen fruited malt loaf
Stem ginger cookies
Tesco Finest Chardonnay white wine vinegar,
  Chianti red wine vinegar
Tesco Ingredients dried ciabatta breadcrumbs,
  piri piri chillies/jalapeño peppers
Tesco ready-toasted pine nuts/flaked almonds,
  traditional Irish wheaten loaf, ditali regati
  dried pasta, tinned green lentils, rosemary
  flaked sea salt
Thai Taste red curry paste, shredded kaffir lime leaves,
  Panang red curry paste
Tinned wild salmon
Tiptree lemon curd, organic hot English mustard
Tracklements chilli jam
Vahiné caramel sauce
Waitrose borettane onions, ready-toasted pine nuts
  ready-toasted flaked almonds, dried festoni pasta
Waitrose Cooks' Ingredients dried breadcrumbs ,
  puttanesca mix, piri piri chillies/jalapeño peppers
Whole Earth crunchy organic peanut butter,
  tomato ketchup

fridge.

Aperi Quail hardboiled quail eggs
Asda ruby red salad, ready-grated Gruyère
Delouis Fils fresh mayonnaise
Fresh, ready-made vanilla custard
Hot smoked salmon fillets
Jus-Rol large shortcrust pastry case, pastry lid
M&S diced feta with olive oil and oregano
M&S chunky guacamole
Marine Gourmet Morecambe Bay potted shrimps
Mr Crumb fresh breadcrumbs
Ready-cooked crispy smoked bacon
Ready-cooked chicken breasts
Ready-dressed Cromer crab
Ready-grated Parmesan
Ready-made fresh gnocchi
Ready-made thin pancakes
Ready-prepared fresh cheese sauce
Ready-prepared fresh pineapple/mango chunks
Ready-prepared shredded cabbage, cauliflower and
    broccoli florets, diced swede and carrot
Sainsbury's fresh Italian three-cheese sauce,
    sliced smoked pancetta, spinach and ricotta
    tortelloni, ready-grated mozzarella and Cheddar
Sainsbury's Taste the Difference Sicilian sausages,
    Sunblush tomatoes
Tesco fresh pesto sauce, ready-grated Gruyère
    cheese, sliced smoked pancetta, ready-grated
    mozzarella and Cheddar
Tesco Finest prawn cocktail, wild mushroom sauce
Waitrose fresh organic coconut chunks, Portobello
    mushroom & Madeira sauce, amaranth &
    watercress salad
Watercress, spinach and rocket leaf salad

freezer.

Asda chargrilled aubergine slices, Morello
    cherries, ready-prepared rhubarb, summer
    fruit berries, Thai curry mix, wild mushroom risotto
Aunt Bessie's Homestyle crispy roast potatoes,
    Homestyle mashed potato
Baby broad beans
Baby squid
Icelandic cod or haddock
Jus-Rol shortcrust pastry sheet, individual puff
    pastry rounds
McCain potato rosti, crispy bites, crispy slices, lightly
    spiced oven-ready wedges, sea salt & black
    pepper wedges
Mixed seafood/fruits de mer
Odysea authentic Greek pitta bread
Parsnips
Plaice fillets
Roeless scallops
Raw tiger or king prawns
Sainsbury's Black Forest fruits, ready-prepared
    rhubarb, summer fruit berries, tropical fruit,
    smoothie mix
Tesco Black Forest fruits, Bramley apple and
    blackberry, Greek farmed sea bass fillets
Tesco Finest Australian snapper fillets
Tesco Whole Foods cooked chickpeas,
    cooked kidney beans
Waitrose artichoke hearts, British garden fruits,
    brown rice, butternut squash, Cornish mackerel
    fillets, Greek farmed sea bass fillets, organic thin &
    crispy stone-baked pizza base, wild salmon and
    seafood medley

stockists.

www.amazon.co.uk
for the Kenwood mini-chopper and Braun 300W
stick blender

www.belazu.com
020 8838 9670
for preserved lemons and other Mediterranean
products

www.butleyorfordoysterage.co.uk
01394 450277
for smoked chipolatas and other smoked products

Carrs Flour Mills
www.breadflour.co.uk
01697 331661
for Carrs sauce flour and other flours

www.camisa.co.uk
01992 763076
for Martelli and Col Sapori di Napoli pasta,
Fruttibosco porcini and antipasto, and other
good-quality authentic Italian and selected how to
cheat ingredients

www.donaldrussell.com
01467 629666
for excellent beef, lamb, pork and game

www.dressitalian.com
020 7352 7250
for Italian sauces and pesto

www.englishprovender.com
01635 528800
for very lazy ginger/caramelised red onions

James Baxter & Son
01524 410910
for Morecambe Bay potted shrimps to freeze

www.janeasher.com
020 7584 6177
for pink chocolate buttons

www.lakeland.co.uk
01539 488100
for good-quality cookware including the Kenwood
mini-chopper and polythene lidded pudding
basins. Specialist ingredients, including spices from
Seasoned Pioneers, Ndali Fairtrade vanilla extract,
Vahiné caramel sauce and Coco López cream
of coconut.

www.lanefarm.co.uk
01379 384593
for good-quality Suffolk pork, bacon and sausages.

Marine Stewardship council
www.msc.org
for information on sustainably fished seafood and
availability

www.maroque.co.uk
01449 723133
for Belazu preserved lemons and other Moroccan
ingredients

www.MorecambeBayShrimps.com
015395 59544
for Morecambe Bay potted shrimps

www.merchant-gourmet.com
020 7635 4096
for Sunblush tomatoes and other gourmet products

www.mothersgarden.org
email: mothersgarden.es@gmail.com
0034 977 178 346
for premium Spanish olive oil direct
from Spain

www.odysea.com
020 7796 1166
for meze, frozen pitta bread and other Greek and
Mediterranean products

www.onlinefoodhall.com
01635 254249
for English Provender caramelised red onions

www.porterfoods.co.uk
01279 501711
for Dress Italian pasta sauces and pesto

www.seasonedpioneers.co.uk
0800 0682348
for spice mixes and curry powders

www.seewoo.com
0845 076 8888
for a wide range of Oriental foods

www.theasiancookshop.co.uk
01376 349009
for a selection of Asian ingredients

www.thedrinkshop.com
0800 169 6760
for Coco López cream of coconut

www.thegoodfoodnetwork.co.uk
020 8466 7170
for Perard fish, crab, lobster soups; Odysea products

www.thespiceshop.co.uk
020 7221 4448
for superior spices, herbs and flavourings

www.tiptree.com
01621 815407
for lemon curd, organic hot English mustard and
other high-quality British preserves and jams

www.tracklements.co.uk
01666 827044
for strong horseradish sauce. chilli jam and other
condiments and preserves

Twineham Grange Farms
01444 881394
for vegetarian Parmesan-style cheese

www.deliaonline.com
for latest news on product availability

Delia's Canary Catering
www.deliascanarycatering.com
General enquiries regarding Delia's Canary
Catering and to book events or Delia's food and
wine workshops, call 01603 218 704
    Mon-Fri, 8am-6pm, Sat 9am-2pm
Delia's Restaurant & Bar Bookings 01603 218 705
    Mon-Thurs 8am-8pm, Fri-Sat until 11pm
Yellows Bookings 01603 218 209
    Mon-Sat 10am-11pm, Sun 11am-10pm
www.yellowsdiner.com

SUPERMARKETS

www.ocado.com
www.waitrose.com
www.tesco.com
www.sainsburys.co.uk
www.asda.co.uk

index

V.

W.